*This book
is dedicated
with profound love and respect
to my daughter
Joan Eileen Murray*

"I am a speculator
so my children
can be dancers."

–Keynes

GATHERING ASSETS

The Best of Nick Murray

BY
NICK MURRAY

Publisher
Robert A. Stanger & Co.
Shrewsbury, New Jersey

Other Publications from Robert A. Stanger & Co.

Periodicals:

THE STANGER REPORT: A GUIDE TO PARTNERSHIP INVESTING
THE STANGER REVIEW: PARTNERSHIP SALES SUMMARY

Books:

SERIOUS MONEY: THE ART OF MARKETING MUTUAL FUNDS
HOW TO EVALUATE REAL ESTATE PARTNERSHIPS

Published by Robert A. Stanger & Co.
1129 Broad St., Shrewsbury, New Jersey 07702

Printed in the United States of America.

Library of Congress Catalog Card Number: 94-74929
ISBN 0-943570-12-3

Contents

Contents

Introduction

Since my book *Serious Money: The Art of Marketing Mutual Funds* was published in the Autumn of 1991, I've gotten pleasantly accustomed to having industry professionals thank me for the book, and even say that it's changed their careers.

So, about a year ago, I sat up and took notice when the nature of this feedback began to change perceptibly. "Loved your column last month," someone would say; "I used your postage stamp idea (or whatever) and landed a huge order. Oh, and I like your book, too."

These references were to a column I'd been writing each month for "Investment Advisor" magazine. At first, these columns were just excerpts from *Serious Money* that were run to drum up interest in the book. But even after *Serious Money* became a huge best seller (the 100,000th copy came off the press in December '94), I found that there were new things I wanted to add—and the column offered an excellent format.

I'm happy to offer, in this book, my favorites from among these columns. This compilation starts with the column from October, 1990 ("Selling Skills for Recessionary Times") in which I more or less inadvertently called the bottom of the market. The actual low was recorded on October 11, my 47th birthday and almost exactly the day that month's issue of the magazine came out. The book ends four years later in October, 1994 with a column taken from my closing keynote speech to the '94 IAFP Convention, "Core Beliefs of the Twenty-First Century Asset Gatherer."

Throughout, these columns develop several recurring themes:

★ A relentless long-term bullishness (tempered late in

'93 by the piece called "Getting Ready For the Fall,"
which was, unfortunately, also right);

★ A profound belief in the investment professional's
capacity to do good for his clients, together with a
passionate advocacy of our right to be fairly compensated for doing so;

★ A consistent call for the re-definition of investment
risk and safety in terms of purchasing power, and an
ongoing plea for the increased equity exposure that
such re-definition requires in American portfolios.

I hope you'll find that all these very serious themes
are liberally sprinkled with real humor (see especially
"The No-Load Cardiologist"), as well as with actual
scripts that make it easier for you to communicate with
your clients in real-life terms.

* * *

During the four years of my association with
"Investment Advisor" magazine—at first under the aegis
of *Serious Money* publisher Bob Stanger, and now with
Barry Vinocur at the helm—my esteem for the magazine
has grown steadily. Today, I believe it's the finest publication of its kind, and an indispensable resource for the
professional asset gatherer. A subscription to "Investment
Advisor" is free to qualified industry professionals. To
subscribe, call 908-389-8700, extension 110.

Selling Skills For Recessionary Times

I've always felt that good people in our business pick up market share in adverse times—that the amateur's "bear market" is the professional's "big sale." When the Saddam Hussein Memorial Instant Recession Massacree hit us in the summer of '90, I was startled by the extent of the resultant paralysis...until I realized just how large a percentage of the industry had never seen a recession.

Though this column strikes me, in retrospect, as surprisingly transaction-oriented (in that it talks a lot more about individual stocks than I usually do), it also strikes me as being marvelously accurate. PepsiCo nearly doubled from the October '90 lows. AMR did double, because Eastern and Pan Am did disappear and TWA downsized in a prolonged and painful bankruptcy. The interest rate on the long bond did crater—although here I literally didn't foresee half the decline. I said that if the recession was really a corker, the yield would go from 9% to 7%; three years later it was actually 5.75%.

But the thing I'm proudest of in this piece was the (sort of) "call" on the market low. After noting that the average postwar recession lasted 10-11 months, and that the stock market bottoms right around the mid-point of the recession, I wrote, "So if we're in a three-to-four quarter recession that...started around July 1, 1990, you'd be looking for the market to be bottoming...just about any time now."

Which, on October 11, at Dow 2450, is exactly what it did.

But my point isn't that your future in the business (or even mine, for that matter) has anything to do with calling market turns. Instead, I was trying to establish that the more you have a sense of the cycle—and of the way the cycle always reasserts itself—the more calmly and clearly you can identify the opportunities in each apocalypse du jour.

Selling Skills For Recessionary Times

If the United States wasn't already in a recession the day before the tanks rolled into Kuwait, you can just about bet the ranch that we're in one now.

With economic growth slowing to zero, employment growth doing likewise, construction spending in the deep-freeze and a credit crunch/banking crisis to boot, you had to know back in July that the economy was going nowhere fast.

Now add a good old-fashioned oil shock to the system, and, after an unprecedented eight-year economic expansion, you've got just what you'd expect: recession.

Right now, a shell-shocked financial services industry is asking: What's happened? And what do we do now? Let's take those two questions in order.

Question: WHAT HAPPENED?

Answer: THE INEVITABLE.

Just because we went eight years without a recession, and had ourselves the longest economic expansion since World War II, didn't mean the cycle got suspended. The economy was just robust enough to keep shaking off tacklers, and it stayed on its feet longer than anybody would have guessed possible.

But trees do not grow all the way to the sky. The cycle always reasserts itself. And, with its massive debt levels, crashing real estate and crippled banking system, the economy needed to lay down and bleed awhile. Which it was in the process of doing—all the talk about a "soft landing" notwithstanding—when oil blindsided it. Pull out of a softening economy all those incremental dollars that have to go for energy, and you're in Recession City.

Thank goodness. Because, as I said, it had to happen sooner or later. And because the financial markets have now adjusted to reality.

You see, when the market was struggling to break 3000, the whole financial community was standing in a corner, fists clenched and eyes shut tight with fear saying, "Please no recession...please no recession..." over and over again. We were in a market that was hoping against hope.

But now the bubble has burst, and reality has set in. Now we can start using everything we know about how markets behave in a recession to make smart investment decisions for our clients...and to get lots of new clients from salespeople who have no memory of a recession and no idea what to do now that we're in one. (You'll find it's relatively easy to open accounts with people whose previous financial advisor has gone into a long-term catatonic state.)

Remember that about 40% of the stockbrokers and financial planners in the business today came in since 1982. In other words, since the last recession. They've lived through some terrific market shocks, to be sure, but never a real recession: two or more quarters of negative GNP growth. Lots of these folks have absolutely no idea what to tell people. So, if you have *any* idea what to tell people, you've already got a leg up on a big chunk of your competition.

What I'd be telling them is this:

1. RECESSIONS DON'T USUALLY LAST ALL THAT LONG. There've been eight recessions since WWII; the average lasted between 10 and 11 months. (Knock out the longest—17 months—and the shortest—5 months—and the average doesn't move.) Putting aside the question of how deep they are, just focus on the fact that recessions are relatively short-lived.

2. ALL STOCKS GET KILLED IN A RECESSION. BUT ALL COMPANIES DON'T. There are lots of companies that are actually recession-resistant. But when the whole market gets routed, these stocks tend to get equally mangled. Few things are more recession-proof than soft drinks, but PepsiCo plunged 26% in August and September. Food stocks and drug stocks also show up in the bargain basement for no reason when recession shakes the stock market.

2

3. IN A RECESSION, SHAKY INDUSTRIES CONSOLIDATE. BUY THE OBVIOUS POTENTIAL SURVIVORS. What industry gets double-whammied by recession and higher oil prices? Airlines, of course. AMR Corp., parent of American Airlines, is now the largest privately-owned airline company in the world. So it's going to get hurt, right? Sure, but lots of weaker players are going to be mortally wounded. Who's going to emerge bigger and stronger if Eastern, TWA or Pan Am says sayonara? American. Meanwhile, the stock's down from 107 to (at this writing) the low-40s. Earnings, shmearnings: it's selling for 30% below book value and less than three times cash flow. What more do you want, frequent flyer mileage with your stock certificate?

4. THE MORE BEARISH YOU ARE ON STOCKS, THE MORE FIXED-INCOME INVESTMENTS I CAN SELL YOU. You call people, and they are howling, screaming bears on stocks. "This market's going to 1600; I'm not buying anything!" Wait now: if you believe that, you're not buying any *stocks*; I can live with that. But I can't sit by idly and let you ignore the chance to more than double your money in the highest quality security known to man.

Got your attention? Here's how it works. If you think the market has the potential to go down almost 50% (from 3000 last June to 1600), you're looking for an economic slowdown of massive proportions—the worst post-war recession yet. ("Darn tootin' I am!" says Mr. Bear.)

Well, in that scenario, interest rates are going to crater. Either they're going to free-fall of their own weight because there's no demand for credit, or the Fed will push 'em down to try to re-start the economy's heart.

Either way, in your scenario, the 30-year U.S. Treasury bond is going to go from yielding 9% to yielding 7% maximum. You can buy Treasurys on 10% margin. Do the math: on a 200 basis point drop, you make nearly two and a half times your equity. Can I buy you $1 million worth, Mr. Bear?

That's the great thing about this profession, there's no such thing as no sale. Tell me why you won't buy what I asked you to buy, and you've told me what you will buy. This same basic argument works perfectly well, if not quite as dramatically, with all bonds, CDs, and fixed annuities.

5. ABOUT HALFWAY THROUGH A RECESSION, THE MARKET STARTS "LOOKING ACROSS THE VALLEY" AND DISCOUNTING THE BEGINNING OF THE NEXT ECONOMIC EXPANSION. The market doesn't start going up after a recession ends; it's the other way around. Remember that the market tends to be discounting on reality six months out. So if we're in a three-to-four quarter recession that, for argument's sake, started around July 1, 1990, you'd be looking for the market to be bottoming...just about any time now. Meanwhile, the headlines are still full of recession.

Now for the answer to the second question.

Question: WHAT DO I DO NOW?

Answer: GET MORE MONEY IN THE HOUSE.

This is not, particularly for commissioned salespeople, a time when you can make quantum changes in your income. But you can make quantum changes in the money you have under control...because people are so frightened and because, rightly or wrongly, they feel so betrayed by their current advisers. (Nobody comes right out and says, "You should have told me Iraq was going to invade Kuwait," but, subconsciously that's what they're all thinking.)

If you can't sell anything else, sell safe havens. Again, anything you do in the fixed-income area is probably going to look pretty good before too long. But that isn't the point.

In one week last August, $6.5 billion went into money market funds, pushing money fund assets over $400 billion for the first time ever. When that money comes out of hiding, it's going to make some planners and salespeople very happy.

You could be among them—if you act now.

Why You Should Be Bullish, Too!

This column was written in the last days of December, 1990. It may be hard to remember now, but retail investors (and a surprising percentage of their institutional counterparts) were in a state of complete paralysis at that time.

The allies had given Saddam Hussein a deadline of January 15 to pull out of Kuwait...and he had indicated that he wasn't going anywhere.

Investors were doing nothing "until we see if war starts"...the universal assumption being that if war started, the equity markets would plunge to new lows.

*As usual, the consensus didn't just have the answer wrong, **it had the question framed badly.** It turned out that the issue wasn't the onset of war, but whether, if the shooting started, Saddam would be able to use his Scud missiles to take out the Saudi oilfields. When, about an hour into the war, it became clear that he couldn't take out the garbage, the market exploded on the upside, gaining 700 Dow points in 7 weeks.*

This article said, in effect, that all the prevalent major investment themes were positive, and that Desert Shield (as it was still called then) wasn't major. (It also, if you'll forgive my saying so, made a great call on the imminent resurgence of the banking industry.)

This stuff may all sound like ancient history, but it happened just four years ago. And if the universal paralysis attendant upon Desert Shield seems silly now, try remembering it when the next apocalypse du jour pulls into town.

So remember my single favorite sentence from this article:

"ALL GREAT BULL MARKETS ARE PHOENIX-LIKE: THEY RISE FROM THE ASHES OF GREAT DESTRUCTION."

Why You Should Be Bullish, Too!

As 1991 begins, the battle-hardened veterans with whom I've grown up in the business are feeling very embattled. Their businesses are down substantially, and they see the current negative trend continuing.

When they asked for my perspective, I'm forced to blurt out the truth: I'm about as bullish as I've ever been in my life. Here's why.

1. In case you hadn't noticed, the greatest political, social and economic struggle in the history of mankind is now over.

In the three-quarters of a century since the Russian Revolution, an untold amount of the world's wealth and energy, as well as millions of lives, have been lost in the struggle between democratic capitalism and totalitarian socialism. During the last year, this titanic battle ended.

It gives me great pleasure to remind you that the good guys won. The whole world now wants to pursue economic incentives under free, democratic governments. We invented both of those concepts. And we will be exporting our capital, technologies and know-how far into the next century.

The Pizza Huts in Moscow are no fluke. Just when American business is coming face to face with the maturing of the American economy, the prospect of global growth emerges. That's very bullish.

Our *USA Today*/six o'clock news mentality tends to focus on the Middle East as the predominant world issue of the day. But peace among the superpowers and the conversion of the world's economy to capitalism will be the great themes of the 1990s. Contrast super-power relationships with 1950—the year my family got a TV set. We used to watch A-bomb tests in the Nevada Desert, broadcast live. For the first time since then, it seems extremely unlikely

7

that the world will disappear in a thermonuclear holocaust. Call me a cock-eyed optimist, but I view this as a positive.

2. America Is De-Leveraging.

Today, virtually no debt market exists for financial takeovers and real estate development. Even two years ago, this would have been akin to saying: There is no oxygen.

The inflated paper "wealth" that proliferated in the past ten years, and the financial system that created it, are in liquidation. The banking system is being wrung out as in no other period since the 1930s. The system will ultimately emerge smaller, consolidated into far fewer and stronger entities, smarter, much better managed, leaner, cleaner and far more conservative. You can focus on the fact (which I don't deny) that this process is far from finished. Or you can focus, as I do, on where the banking system will be when the process is complete.

Meanwhile, people's expectations are becoming more realistic. The "wealth effect" of dizzyingly soaring home prices is evaporating. And so is the willingness of people to borrow ever more money because their house is making them a zillionaire. Reality has set in, and reality is invariably bullish in the long run because people will lever down and rebuild reserves.

And speaking of reserves...

3. A staggering, unprecedented amount of cash is poised on the sidelines.

Look at the trend of money market fund assets in Figure 1. For the first time in the history of money funds, assets exceed $400 billion.

Not only that, but the cash position of equity mutual funds recently hit an all-time high. At the end of October, cash hit 12.9% of assets in equity mutual funds—a level never seen before. At the bottom of the '69-70 bear market, cash was 10.1%. In the debacle of '73-74, cash never topped 11.8%.

4. Short interest is at an all-time high.

Both the New York Stock Exchange and NASDAQ reported all-time record short positions in November. This is fascinating,

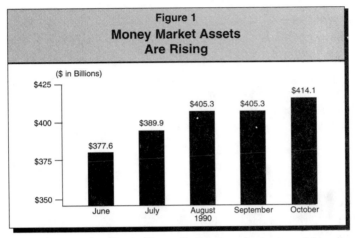

Figure 1
Money Market Assets
Are Rising

($ in Billions)

June: $377.6
July: $389.9
August 1990: $405.3
September: $405.3
October: $414.1

because almost nobody shorts well. So, for a huge bearish consensus to have built up to record amounts of short-selling, you have to wonder if a bottom is at hand. Of course, I have no idea how close we are to the bottom, either in price or time. I just know we're an awful lot closer than the consensus thinks.

5. The economy is finally in a meaningful downturn.

Whether you're in a classically defined "recession" (two quarters of negative GNP growth) remains to be seen. But if not, the economy is doing a great recession imitation.

Moreover, Alan Greenspan has acknowledged that the economy is going south. And he's the guy who has to press the button on meaningfully lower interest rates. Remember, a substantial drop in interest rates is what economic recoveries—and bull markets—are made of.

After eight years of precarious economic expansion, fueled by insane debt creation, we need this downturn. Now we're in it. But the recession won't last all that long. The average postwar recession has been 10 to 11 months long and has ended when interest rates cratered.

6. The number of NYSE-registered reps is in free-fall.

I'm sorry, but all my experience tells me that the number of stockbrokers varies inversely with the health of the market. Here's a table of the number of stockbrokers working at NYSE-member firms over the last decade. Look at the 10% surge in the nine months just before the greatest stock market crash of all time, and you'll see what I mean.

I don't minimize the human damage involved in this downturn, any more than I do the financial dislocation. But all great bull markets are phoenix-like: they rise from the ashes of great destruction.

Hang in there. The bear market is weakening, even if it does have one more savage attack left in it...which it may.

But when the bear finally backs off, you may be looking at a golden age. Make sure you're still here.

Stockbrokers With NYSE-Member Firms	
Date	**Reps**
March 1979	46,608
Dec. 1984	78,369
Dec. 1986	88,380
March 1987	94,031
June 1987	92,956
Sept. 1987	96,583
Dec. 1987	92,282
March 1988	90,260
June 1988	88,743
Sept. 1988	87,793
Dec. 1988	87,650
March 1989	86,001
June 1989	83,601
Sept. 1989	82,468
Dec. 1989	80,908
March 1990	78,153
June 1990	76,871

Rx For Equity Jitters: Sell Dividend Growth

One of my core beliefs is that the great financial risk in American life in the next century won't be losing your money, but outliving it. For people who have to plan for 25 to 30 years of retirement, therefore, their primary investment goal shouldn't be either "growth" or "income" but growth *of* income. And no income stream grows as steadily or as much as the dividends from The Great Companies in America. In this article, I suggested that

"...GROWTH OF DIVIDENDS.. IS TO INFLATION WHAT ST. GEORGE WAS TO THE DRAGON."

I've noticed that the same Americans who think stocks kill you believe that the owners of great businesses get rich. So I talk about companies or businesses, rather than about stocks. And the same people who don't believe that stock prices go up do believe that great companies make more money over time, and therefore increase their dividends.

Voila! Mr. & Mrs. Risk-Averse Investor, allow me to present St. George...

Rx For Equity Jitters: Sell Dividend Growth

Quick! What's the thing about owning common stocks that people hate the most? Right! Sudden, unpredictable downdrafts in the stocks' prices (sometimes inaccurately referred to as risk).

Now, what's the thing about common stocks that people love most? Right again: the dividend. And particularly the fact that, every once in a while, good companies raise their dividend.

And yet, I'll bet that 99 out of 100 planners out there are still relentlessly basing their equity mutual fund sales presentations solely on the idea of price appreciation.

You're ignoring the simple but sage advice of old-time baseball great "Wee" Willie Keeler. Asked for the secret of a superior batting average, Willie invariably replied, "Hit 'em where they ain't."

People have a hard time believing in price appreciation these days. After nearly half a decade of unprecedented volatility in common stock prices, the great mass of investors have trouble relating the prices of stocks to the values of companies. The stock market has taken on the air of a casino, in which arbitrageurs, con men, madmen and crazed computers (performing a satanic ritual called program trading) conspire to destroy the individual investor.

But nobody is ever mad at dividends. So, if you're running into a wall on the issue of the appreciation potential of common stocks, you can restore a sense of rationality to client interviews by focusing on dividends. And most particularly on the inexorable growth of dividends, which is to inflation what St. George was to the dragon.

People Need Equities

Let's review the bidding. First, we know that equities are the only financial asset which maintain purchasing power, net of inflation and taxes. Today's generation of investors, who are planning to retire earlier and live longer than anybody in history, have decades, not years, of inflation to deal with. Slowly, but surely, they're coming to the realization that the greatest risk they face isn't losing their capital. It's outliving their income. That means people need equities. And boy, do they hate it.

Have a little pity for them. Don't ask them to make a painful and difficult leap of faith and put their confidence in a concept they deeply distrust—price appreciation. Instead, show them how right they are to instinctively love equities' most lovable attribute: dividend growth.

If a picture's worth a thousand words, the accompanying table ought to be worth about a million. It shows the 20-year dividend growth patterns of some of the great stocks most widely held in equity mutual funds today. And it relates that income growth to the erosion of purchasing power implicit in inflation.

Dividend Growth Patterns

Company	Cash Dividend* 1971	Cash Dividend* 1990	# of Years Dividend Raised	20-Year Compound Annual Growth Rate
Mobil Oil	$.60	$2.55	15	7.50%
Warner-Lambert	.29	1.28	ALL	7.64%
IBM	.96	4.73	13	8.30%
General Electric	.34	1.88	19	8.93%
Coca Cola	.12	.68	ALL	9.06%
Pfizer	.32	2.20	ALL	10.18%
PepsiCo	.04	.32	15	11.39%
Philip Morris	.03	1.25	17	19.96%
Consumer Price Index				**6.40%**

*Adjusted for stock splits.

Another benefit you can derive from presenting the concept this way is its specificity. The stock market is a scary abstraction. But, again, nobody's mad at The Great Companies in America. This is a critical distinction, not a semantic one. Whenever you hear a prospect talking about stocks in a fearful or pejorative way, you can change the whole emotional tone of the conversation by talking about companies.

Great companies tend to do better each year, as the American (and, increasingly, the global) economy grows. Moreover, the companies themselves get better. Look at Philip Morris, systematically using its prodigious tobacco cash flow to acquire great food businesses (Kraft, General Foods, Miller Brewing). Or PepsiCo, diversifying from a soft drink company into the most profitable major food company in the world (Frito-Lay) and the largest restaurant chain in the world outside the U.S. (Kentucky Fried Chicken).

As these great companies' earnings increase, shareholders are rewarded for their patience and long-term perspective. The form of that reward: increased dividends, the ultimate inflation-killer.

Use Concrete Examples

When you've selected a favorite growth mutual fund, or a growth and income fund, make it a point to become familiar with the dividend histories of some of the fund's largest holdings. (Your firm's research library or the mutual fund itself can provide you with this information.)

Then, when you're presenting growth of income as the one indispensable benefit that only equities provide, you can refer to one or two very concrete, very comforting examples. People really like it when you've clearly done your homework, and gone beyond the obvious to the subtle reasons why your favorite mutual fund works. This lets clients feel that you have a real understanding of, and commitment to, the particular fund you've chosen for them.

Isolating on dividend growth has the added benefit of giving you the moral high ground in any discussion of risk. Because, in the long run, it is impossible for the price of a stock and the dividend to go in opposite directions for any length of time. Dividend growth signals, in the most concrete way possible, that a company is doing progressively better.

And if a company is doing better over time, the price of the stock may go down once in a while, but it can never stay down. On the contrary, over any meaningful time frame, the price will go in the same direction as the dividend. Even the most risk-averse investor will have to conclude that this is no more or less than common sense.

So stop arguing price appreciation. It's a pop-up to the infield.

"Hit 'em where they ain't" by showing the marvelous dividend histories of the great companies, and how only the growth of income through equities can offset the "growth" of living costs through inflation.

And remember, dividend growth is like Sara Lee: nobody doesn't like it.

The Mother Of All Buy Signals

*This wasn't one of my regular columns at all,
but kind of an "op-ed" piece at the end of the
magazine. The market had soared in 1991, but I
had been amazed to find the public's equity
holdings continuing to fall, as a percentage of
total household financial assets. This was, I
believed, phenomenally bullish for the longer
term, no matter how far the market had come. In
summary, I wrote,*

*"...ANY ASSET CLASS THE
INDIVIDUAL INVESTOR HATES
THIS MUCH WILL GO MUCH,
MUCH HIGHER...PERHAPS
HIGHER THAN MOST OF US
CAN IMAGINE."*

*Two years later, almost to the day, the DJIA
made an intra-day high of 4000, its highest
reading in history...so far.*

The Mother Of All Buy Signals

One year ago, I sent a Christmas message to friends throughout the industry—an article titled "Why You Should Be Bullish Too!" which appeared in the January '91 issue of this magazine. You may not remember how bearish public sentiment was at that time, but most folks were awfully pessimistic. Luckily, I wasn't, and, as it happened, I was right.

At the risk of pushing my luck, look at the graph on this page. No, Santa didn't send it, although he may just as well have. The chart came my way through the courtesy of H. Bradlee Perry, chairman of David L. Babson & Company, the mutual fund and investment advisory group headquartered in Cambridge, Mass.

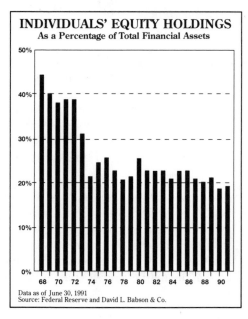

INDIVIDUALS' EQUITY HOLDINGS
As a Percentage of Total Financial Assets

Data as of June 30, 1991
Source: Federal Reserve and David L. Babson & Co.

Put down that eggnog and take a look at the long-term trend in individual investors' equity holdings, including both common stocks and mutual funds. From a peak of about 45% of total financial assets in 1968 (the tippy top of the 20-year, post-war bull market), investors' equity holdings plunged to 20% in the holocaust of 1973-74, when the Dow fell below 600.

Today, the Dow is five times higher, but people are holding an even smaller percentage of assets in equities! (Take a belt of that eggnog, then re-read the preceding sentence.)

Regular readers of my column in this magazine know that I'm a devout believer in the infinite capacity of the individual investor to zig when he should zag. But this aberration is beyond anything I could have imagined. What you see flashing here is not a Christmas "sale" sign in the store window, it's simply…the Mother of All Long-Term Buy Signals!

Like a lot of people, I've long been aware that when it comes to owning individual stocks, the investor is (to use Samuel Goldwyn's classic phrase) "staying away in droves." But I just assumed investors had diverted equity holdings into mutual funds. The chart, however, shows the sum of the two forms of equity holdings. So, 80% of folks' money is someplace else.

The Grinch Factor

This fact should be sobering for those grinches who hold that at current levels of valuation the stock market is intrinsically "too risky," because it's "too high." These are, of course, many of the same people who, a year ago, thought the market was "too risky" because it was "too low"…and going lower. (Murray's Sixth Law of Time & Non-Motion says: The shortest period measurable by man is between the time it's "too soon" to buy stocks and the time it's "too late.")

The "too high" crowd believes the market is "ahead of itself," i.e. far too pricey in terms of the earnings companies can realize in the kind of agonizingly slow economic recovery we seem to be having. By this test, of course, the market was positively astronomical last March. And yet, wonder of wonders, it's even higher now. Could it be that the market knows something we don't know? I'm betting it does.

New Year's Message

Bear Stearns' chief economist Lawrence Kudlow told clients last month, "If you believe, as we do, that markets contain more information than econometric models or economic experts, then the clear message from rising share prices is a prediction of stronger economic growth ahead." He went on to point out that inflation has dropped by roughly 50% from peak rates of between 5% and 7% two years ago.

Short-term interest rates have fallen nearly 50% since the summer of '89, and long-term rates roughly 20%. It's been almost ten years since the last recession turned into the last recovery, so maybe you've forgotten (or just weren't around then). But, at every turning point, you'll always hear a chorus of soothsayers arguing that "rates still aren't low enough"...or even that "lower rates won't stimulate the economy at all." But, as Kudlow notes, "lower rates *always* stimulate the economy." (OK, so I added the italics. You want to make something of it?)

Simultaneously, lower interest rates, lower inflation and rising stock prices have *always* correctly signaled future economic recovery.

But all these economic facts, taken together, don't make me as bullish as that one stark, simple chart, of investors' attitudes toward equities. Everything I've learned in a quarter of a century in this business tells me that any asset class the individual investor hates this much will go much, much higher...perhaps higher than most of us can imagine.

Happy New Year.

The Bear And The Pussycat

Even I don't know what made me turn around, one month after the paean to bullishness you just read, and write a cautionary piece about bear markets. I didn't have any sense that a major correction was imminent. But, in fact, a savage shakeout of the previous year's darlings (small-cap, healthcare, etc.) was just at that moment getting underway. "I hope and expect that this article isn't the least bit timely," I wrote. I was wrong; but maybe, in the process of being wrong, I did somebody some good.

I include this column because of a gnawing fear that it's timely again, as 1995 dawns. The column made the point that the only two bear markets we'd had since '82 were uncharacteristically brief, and that new highs followed very quickly. The message was: bears ain't usually that friendly. And this is a message that just may "bear" repeating.

You see, from September '93 until October '94, the yield on the long bond went up 50%. That's an epic, history-making bear market in bonds. Yet the stock market ended that period right around where it began (albeit with a short, sharp drop in the middle).

*Maybe the other shoe isn't going to drop. On the other hand, maybe it's time to read this column again...**very carefully.***

January, 1992

The Bear And The Pussycat

About half the securities salespeople and financial planners now active in the U.S. entered the business since 1982. We all create investment strategies based primarily on our own experience. So, these nice folks are probably investing in equities (or equity mutual funds), based partly on the assumption that the two bear markets they've seen (1987 and 1990) were pretty typical.

Ursus Minor

Trouble is these declines weren't typical. By many historical standards, they weren't even genuine, sharp-toothed bears—more like pussycats. Table 1 shows you what I mean.

Though very sharp, these declines were extremely short. Moreover, they were overcome very quickly. After the '87 crash, the market went pretty much straight up for more than a year and a half, well into new high ground. The Gulf War/recession massacre of '90 was all but erased by March '91.

My concern is that people may be reasoning as follows: Yes, the market is capable of extreme volatility—plunging tremendously with little or no warning. But, since the long-term trend is up, such declines are merely annoyances—bumpy detours along the inexorable path to ever higher levels. Market advances, in this view, are like the crosstown bus: Be patient, another one will come along in

TABLE 1 Stock Market Declines		
Date of Decline	**Percentage Decline**	**Duration In Days**
1987—August 25 to October 19	36.1%	55
1990—July 16 to October 11	21.2%	87

23

about 15 minutes. Just buy and hold...and relax—this is simple.

Well, "buy and hold" (either with or without dollar-cost-averaging) *is* pretty simple and works over very long holding periods. But, historically, the strategy has been anything but easy. Why? Because most investors just aren't temperamentally suited to the "buy and hold" approach, particularly in a more typical bear market.

Ursus Major

Let's look at the real, fur-covered, carnivorous bears of the postwar period, which appeared when the DJIA declined 20% or more (see Table 2).

TABLE 2		
Fur-Covered, Carnivorous Bears		
Date of Decline	Percentage Decline	Duration In Days
May 29,1946—May 17, 1947	23.2%	353
April 6, 1956—October 22, 1957	19.4%	564
December 13, 1961—June 26, 1962	27.1%	195
December 3, 1968—May 26, 1970	35.9%	539
January 11, 1973—December 6, 1974	45.1%	694
September 21, 1976—February 28, 1978	26.9%	525
April 27, 1981—August 12, 1982	24.1%	472

(Yes, I know I fudged on the 1956-57 bear market, but 19.4% is close enough.)

Not pretty, is it? Don't ask how long you had to wait to get even after some of these debacles—you don't want to know. Just let me suggest that if you went out on the sidewalk on Memorial Day to wait for the bus to Recovery Street, you'd have frozen to death before your foot left the curb. I still have the bite marks from my first run-in with a typical bear—the '68 to '70 market. (By the way, it's true: You never forget your first...bear.) In percentage terms, the '68 to '70 decline was almost exactly the same as the '87 crash...but it took *ten times* longer to happen.

Ok, so maybe everything happens faster these days. (Maybe, as Tom DeVere of Kidder Peabody said, the last 200 points of the Black Monday '87 decline were due to CNN's Titanic/Hindenburg/Hiroshima/End of Life on the Planet news coverage.) But is that a thesis on which you want to bet your clients' retirement money? I hope not.

In the long run, you'd be safer to see the two most recent "pussy-cat" markets as atypical—as a testimony to the tremendous power and resilience of the great bull market that started in the summer of 1982...and is still going on.

Readers of this column know I'm a firm believer in the need for significantly more equity exposure in American portfolios. And you also know that I'm very, very bullish on equities for the next several years. So this is not a warning of impending doom; I hope and expect that this article isn't the least bit timely.

I just want to make sure that your long-term strategies are based on reasonable expectations.

Taming The Bear

When you lead your clients into the cage with the bear (and it's bound to happen at some point, or points, in your career), your chance of survival increases if you've matched the fund manager's style to your client's temperament. Particularly when choosing an equity mutual fund, don't take the easy way out and simply look at five or ten-year relative performance. Life would be a lot easier if you could just look at relative performance and know which fund is "best." Unfortunately, in the real world there are no one-variable questions. So, make sure you know—and your clients know—how the manager handles market declines.

Many equity funds remain more or less fully invested in stocks all the time. The argument is: "That's what you hired us for. If you want to try to time the market, go ahead. But we're in for the very long haul, giving you the opportunity to dollar-cost-average throughout market cycles. If you dollar-cost-average around a rising trendline, given enough time you'll become rich and famous and live forever." As I said: Simple...but, particularly in the crunch, not an easy strategy for most clients to stick with.

Other equity funds raise very significant cash positions during declining markets. This puts a big premium on the manager's ability to be mostly right about the market. But, when the strategy works, it makes a fund's net asset value relatively sticky on the downside.

Is either approach "right" and the other "wrong?" I don't think so. But frankly, I don't much care. The real question is: Which approach are you and your clients most likely to stick with—in bull markets, pussycat markets…and bear markets?

For the last two-thirds of a century, common stocks have provided returns that are roughly double those of long-term bonds, and nearly triple the inflation rate. Stock investing is not easy, but it's worth the work. Just remember to match the fund's management approach with your clients' (and your own) style and temperament…and don't underestimate the bear.

The Wrong And Right Way To Sell Equity Mutual Funds

I guess about the only thing that I hate worse than people not buying equity funds is people buying equity funds for the wrong reasons. In the former instance, people just incur opportunity costs. But in the latter, they almost always lose part of their investment.

Transactional selling of relationship-oriented products is the ultimate square peg in a round hole. Selling equity funds on the basis of a call on the market, or on the illusion of track record, or—worst of all—on current yield, is transaction-oriented, and hence doomed. These approaches always set the investor up to fail.

In this piece, I wrote a five-point mini-presentation of equity funds generically, based on the previously discussed concept of growth of income. I think you'll find it timeless; I know that today, nearly three years after I first wrote out the presentation, I don't feel I need to change a word of it. My favorite lines from this column:

*"…WHEN THE MARKET GOES DOWN, EVEN THE FINEST COMPANIES' STOCKS GO DOWN. **THEY JUST NEVER STAY DOWN."***

The Wrong and Right Way To Sell Equity Mutual Funds

With the market moving higher and the yield on fixed-income investments sagging, sales of equity mutual funds are going strong. And, though it would be great if this sales increase was happening for all the right reasons—that doesn't seem likely.

So, maybe this is a good time to pause and look at the ways we sell equity funds. Because some of the easier sales tracks we're tempted to follow are also, in the long run, the most dangerous. And getting investors to make the right decision for the wrong reasons can be even more injurious (to their finances and your client relationships) than never making the right decision at all. (Once I've covered the three really dumb ways to sell equity funds, I'll turn my attention to the right way to sell them, using five points you can make in under five minutes.)

Three Dumb Ways

Here's a sampling of three of the more common ways we may be encouraging investors to invest in equities, all of which are destined to sooner or later blow up in their—and our—faces. They are: (1) Buy now because the market's going higher; (2) buy now because this fund has a great track record; and (3) buy now because yields on competing instruments stink.

• **Market's Going Higher**—This is a classic technique used by weak salespeople to introduce a false immediacy into the process. Sooner or later, one of two things happens. The investor buys and the market goes down. Or the investor buys, the market goes up and **then** goes down.

By using the false logic that the client should buy because the market's going up, you set the stage for his wanting to get out when (as it inevitably must) the market goes down. Which is the last thing you want to do when the market drops.

Market pullbacks are buying opportunities and an intelligent program of equity investing recognizes that fact. Buying more equity mutual funds makes sense because equities are the only financial asset that consistently preserves purchasing power. Simply put: Equities are the only answer to the problem that fixed-income investing in a rising-cost world is suicide.

Turning the decision to buy an equity mutual fund into a bastardized attempt at market timing totally blurs the critical issue. People need to own more equities because they need to build an income stream that outruns inflation. Sell equities that way—the right way—and they'll stay sold. Sell them as a way to play the market, and it'll come back to haunt you every time.

• **Terrific Track Record**—Admittedly, this isn't quite as bad as the market-timing ploy, but it's right up there.

Track-record selling, like all selling based on alleged "proof," is essentially weak. Moreover, to today's risk-averse investor considering his first serious commitment to equities, it's entirely the wrong appeal.

Track record addresses the issue of return (although what historic return has to do with potential return isn't discussed). But the fledgling fund investor is a lot more concerned with risk than with return. And track record doesn't speak to that concern in any useful way.

The long-term returns from equities are only available to the investor if he stays the long-term course. Track-record selling encourages the investor not to think about the market's downdrafts. Then, when a real downdraft hits, the investor can't keep emotionally afloat on yesterday's track record. So he bails out.

The other thing you have to remember about track record is that every manager's performance goes into eclipse from time to time. Nobody's system works all the time. And the more consistent and disciplined a manager's game plan is, the more certain you can be that it'll go out of sync with the market every so often. If you haven't built up the investor's tolerance for these dry spells, he's going to check out of the fund at exactly the wrong time.

So, forget track record. Concentrate on finding a fund that your investor can be—and stay—comfortable with. Because the more comfortable he is, the more likely he'll stay the course and reap the rewards.

• **Yield**—On any given day, this is arguably the dumbest way to sell anything that's equity related.

The whole point of equities isn't what they yield today, but what that income can grow to tomorrow. Growth of income, at least as fast as your living costs are inflating, is equity's magic bullet. To trivialize that magic by comparing it heads-up to some debt instrument with a static payout is to miss the point entirely. Furthermore, it sets the investor up to stampede out of equities and back into debt the next time interest rates spike (which always causes stocks to swoon).

Any time you tell the investor—even if only by implication—that 7% is better than 5%, and that that's all there is, you've set him on the road to a big mistake. If stocks yielded half what money market funds did, you'd still need to own more of them.

The Right Way

If those are all the wrong ways to sell equity funds, what's the right way? I think there are five points you need to make, and, when you get good at this, you can make them in less than five minutes.

1. **You have to start today to build an income stream that can grow as fast or faster than your living costs grow**. "Growth" is too abstract a concept for the risk-averse investor; he doesn't believe in it. Go with the concept of growth of income; it's the only financial sanity.

2. **In the whole universe of investments, only one financial asset consistently outgrows your living costs.** I call it "owning pieces of good businesses." (You can call it "the stock market," but risk-averse folks translate that phrase to mean "malignant casino.")

I think Americans intuitively know that the people who get wealthy in this country are those who own businesses; the people who get very wealthy are the ones who own great businesses. Forget stocks; talk about owning pieces of successful businesses.

3. **It's critical, as you assemble your portfolio of good business-es, that you hire a first-class institution to manage it.** The market for shares of good businesses in this country has become totally dominated by institutions—more so than at any other time in my 25-year career. The risk-averse investor hasn't got the tools or the emotions to compete; he's got to become an institution, too. (Incidentally, who said anything about "mutual funds"?)

4. **You need, you deserve, and you can well afford the excellent manager I've chosen for you.** Remember: The key issue is that the client understand the manager and be comfortable with his style. Of course, the track record's fine; you'd never recommend a second-rater. But, as we've seen, it's not the platform on which you want to run for election. And, just at the moment, it's the answer to a question nobody's asked.

5. **No investment is perfect; this investment is imperfect in ways you can be comfortable with.** This is a statement of the limitations of the fund you've chosen. For instance, a portfolio of seasoned, big-cap, blue chip stocks isn't going to be up 30% in a year when the market's up 10%.

And when the market goes down, even the finest companies' stocks go down. They just never stay down. Cyclical downturns are part of the game; smart people know these are buying opportunities. The important thing is that you go in with your eyes open.

Make Your Choice

This is one way—not a perfect way, and certainly not the only way, but one way—that real professionals can sell equity funds to real people so that the investor stays sold, through good times and bad.

Sure, it's a tougher sale than any or all of the Three Dumb Ways. But our business is like that. There's no such thing as a sale with no tough part. But you get to pick where you want the tough part to be. Take the easy way now, and you'll get the tough part (with accrued emotional interest) later on when the market hits a pothole. However, if you take the tough part now, it'll pay financial and emotional dividends—to you and the client—for many years to come.

Utility Funds: Entry-Level Equities For The Risk-Averse

I reprint this article here because, after the massacre that utility stocks went through in 1994, I believe they represent great long-term value again.

The basic presentation to the individual investor remains the same: your utility bills go up all the time, and the utility company's shareholders get higher dividends all the time...for the same reasons. Unless you plan to spend the rest of your life tending the campfire, you have no choice but to be involved in this transaction. The question is, which side do you want to be on?

*Again, though, one word of caution: selling utility funds on their current yield is a one-way ticket to Palookaville. Utilities are everybody's entry-level education in the miracle of dividend **growth**. As the article says,*

"TODAY'S YIELD CAN NEVER BE THE POINT, HERE. IT'S TOMORROW'S YIELD THAT COUNTS."

Utility Funds: Entry-Level Equities For The Risk-Averse

Bombarded by negative reports about the economy, most risk-averse investors remain paralyzed. Having missed out on the steep rise in equity prices over the last year and a half, and with the economic recovery (which the market has been correctly forecasting all this time) clearly upon us, these investors look at the market and say: "It's too late."

Well, there's a wonderful equity investment for which it's really never too late. Moreover, it's a very comfortable entry-level equity investment for the fixed-income investor who's gotten creamed by cratering interest rates. It is, of course, mutual funds specializing in utility stocks.

A Very Sweet Track Record

If anything, you have to be careful how you present utility funds to the suspicious and shell-shocked risk-averse investor. That's because the performance of utility stocks has been so good for so long that the track record may send the guy into insulin shock. Try some of these numbers on for size:

• For the ten years ending December 31, 1991, the compound average annual return of the S&P Utility Average was 20%...compared to 17.7% for the S&P 500!

• What's that you say? I'm sandbagging you by picking a period of declining interest rates and inflation? You'll have to try harder than that. Because, over the 20 years to year-end 1991 (encompassing the runaway inflation/skyrocketing interest-rate 1970s), the S&P Utility index produced a 13.5% compound average annual return, vs. 12% for the S&P 500!

More Than First Meets The Eye

You don't have to believe (and I don't contend) that utility stocks are guaranteed to continue outperforming industrials. (Climb out on that limb, and the skeptical investor will saw it off for you, right quick.) But I think these numbers tell you that utilities are far from a punk investment, and that maybe you should be paying a lot more attention to them. I also think the key to utility stocks' attractiveness isn't quite what it first appears, and this becomes the basis of an effective presentation to a nervous investor.

You see, more and more people are realizing that the greatest financial risk they face is outliving their income. But as soon as you try to show them that equities are the only effective financial antidote, investors go back into the mode "No-I-don't-want-to-lose-my-money." And they stay in fixed-income investments. So the classic strength of utilities dovetails beautifully with the investor's deepest need; not income, but growth of income. That's how you sell utility funds.

If your living costs are going to keep going up for the rest of your life, you'd better have an investment portfolio whose income rises steadily, too. (In a rising-cost world, fixed-income investing is a treadmill to oblivion.) And few investments have as fine a record of steadily (if unspectacularly) raising their dividends as do utility stocks.

Please notice that I'm pointedly not suggesting that you sell the absolute level of a utility fund's income vs. the absolute level of, say, bond yields. You can get away with that in the short run (e.g., now), but long term it's a dead end. Today's yield can never be the point, here. It's tomorrow's yield that counts. Let me show you what I mean.

I looked at one large utility fund which had a 5.2% current yield in 1987. If you'd run up against an investor just looking at the absolute level of current income, and you'd shown him that fund, you'd have been dead meat. But if the guy had bought that fund at the beginning of '87, and reinvested the dividends, his current yield on his original investment would have been around 9.3% in 1991...the year interest rates went to the South Pole, and then fell off the face of the earth. Again: focus on growth of income as the ultimate inflation killer, and you'll be a hero.

Some More Definite Pluses

Before putting together a sample presentation, let's look at a couple of other big things you've got going for you when you talk about utilities to a risk-averse investor.

• **He's Familiar With Them.** Investors who worry a lot always fall back on what psychologists call their "affiliation needs." That is, they tend to focus on what their friends are doing, just because they're groping for familiarity. Trouble is, the consensus of their friends is always wrong. Utilities give you a chance to serve up a lot of familiarity with a more positive spin on the ball, as we'll see in the presentation.

• **Stability.** Utilities aren't much affected by the waxing and waning of the economic cycle…along with your mortgage, your bills for electricity, gas, and the phone are about the last bills you wouldn't pay, no matter what other purchases you had to postpone. (Please note that we're using "stability" here to describe a utility's recession resistance. DO NOT use it to say that utility stocks are "less volatile." Stay way from the "V" word altogether, please; it makes people very nervous.) So here's the presentation:

Superstar: Mr. Prospect, which way have your utility bills been going in the last few years: up, down, sideways?

Prospect: Are you kidding? They go up almost every month.

Superstar: Sure, mine too. Think that means utility companies are making more money?

Prospect: Of course they are.

Superstar: Exactly right. Now, who owns utility companies?

Prospect: I don't know…the stockholders, I guess.

Superstar: Right again. In fact, your whole analysis of this situation is right on target; you pay more and more to the utilities; they make more and more money; so they pay higher and higher dividends to their shareholders. Of all the parties to this situation, who's got far and away the best deal?

Prospect: The stockholders, of course!

Superstar: Bingo. (Silence)

Prospect: Tell me what you're getting at.

Superstar: I think you've already figured it out, but I'll be happy to spell it out for you. For safety, stability, high current income and, most important, income that grows every year, nothing beats utility stocks. Nothing.

Prospect: Which utility stocks should I buy?

Superstar: Beats me; I'm not very good at picking individual stocks. Besides, I think the three cardinal rules of investing are: diversify, diversify, diversify. So I just hire a professional investment manager who specializes in utility stocks, and he goes out and buys my clients a whole portfolio of good utilities. And how do you know they're the good ones? Because, nearly every time you turn around, your dividend check goes up. Or at least it sure seems like that.

Prospect: Who are these guys?

Superstar: Glad you asked. (Then he rolls right into the 5-minute, 5-point fund presentation you'll find in my book *Serious Money: The Art of Marketing Mutual Funds.*)

Signalling A Buying Opportunity

One last point. I said that utilities are timeless. And they are. But right now, utility stocks are flashing a signal that reliably shows them to be a better buy than utility bonds. And that signal usually (not always, but usually) brings out renewed institutional buying of utility stocks.

You see, during the first week in April, the yield on the average electric utility common stock ticked up to 7.0%, which was 78% of the roughly 8.9% long-term AA-rated electric utility bond yield. And, anytime electric utility common stock yields are more than 75% of long-term utility bonds, many institutions believe the common stocks are more attractive.

So, do what the smart institutions are doing—take another look at utility common stocks and the great funds that buy them.

Stop Selling, Start Redefining

Around the middle of 1992, I really started to pound away at the self-destructive way in which Americans define "risk" and "safety"—purely in terms of principal, just the way their mom and dad taught 'em to do.

*Americans were acculturated by an episode of deflation, the same as Argentinians were acculturated by a lifetime of inflation. The trouble is that deflation is an anomaly. It's the opposite of reality, just like a compass that points south if you stand in one particular spot. Between the '29 Crash and the end of 1932, the Consumer Price Index actually fell 24%. The currency not only stored value, but **gained** value.*

This led Americans to enshrine the currency, and any investment that was "guaranteed," at the end of its life, to turn back into exactly the same number of pictures of George Washington you traded for it.

This article recommends several different approaches/scripts, all based on new and healthier definitions of risk, safety and income…in real, rather than nominal, terms.

At times like this, when the banks are starting to run ads for (and I quote) "NO RISK CDs," this issue of redefining vs. selling is worth looking at again.

Stop Selling, Start Redefining

This month marks the tenth anniversary of the greatest bull market in the history of both stocks and bonds. It is only natural, then, that as we look about us we see our clients' and prospects' financial plans being destroyed as never before.

HUH?!? How is that possible? What kind of sense does that make?

Actually, it makes all the sense in the world. Because in this decade, we, as an industry, have completely shattered our lances against the impenetrable shield of our clients' definitions.

If, and to the extent that, our clients' financial plans are turning to dust and blowing away on the wind, it isn't because we sold badly. (I actually think we're selling better today than we ever did, not that that's saying much.) It's because our clients defined the issues so badly, and we weren't able to stop them.

Savaged By Their Definitions

Indeed, two whole classes of investors—which together include just about everybody you meet these days—have been savaged by their definitions.

First is the investor who was attempting to accumulate capital by buying fixed-income investments and reinvesting the income. He defined the compounding of income as "growth"…and fell on not one sword, but three: (1) taxes, (2) inflation, and (3) cratering interest rates. Net net, this guy literally doesn't have the same purchasing power he had ten years ago. Why? Bad definitions.

The other, and even more obvious, victim of toxic definitions is the investor who has been relying on his short-term debt investments for "safety" and "income." This guy has, through the iron force of the way he defined those terms, managed to become quite literally destitute. His cost of living is up about 40% in the last ten years, and his income—from CDs, money markets and Treasuries—is down about 75%. (Incidentally, the highly respected Ned Davis Research firm estimates that there is about *four trillion dollars* of household financial assets in this category.)

Fatal Blows

These nice folks made two distinct definitional errors, either one of which would have been critical, but both together are invariably fatal.

First, they mistook "certainty" for "safety." This is a misnomer left over from the Great Depression, which was, of course, the mother of all deflations. It leads to a psychology that says, "Above all, if I can't lose my principal, I am safe."

Trouble is, you're not safe at all. You're in mortal danger from inflation, the slow, inevitable, inexorable grinding down of your purchasing power, which must attend upon even the smallest annual price increases. And the ultimate irony is that the "safer" your principal is, the more insulated from growth it is, and the more you get ravaged by inflation.

The twin of this toxic definition is "income." Again, the issue is the inability to distinguish between nominal interest rates and real interest rates. So the "safety and income" crowd was never happier than in 1981, when six-month CD rates averaged 15.77%. (As the immortal Casey Stengel said, "You could look it up.") Never mind that, net of double-digit inflation and a combined tax rate of at least 40%, they were way underwater. Those niceties are outside the scope of their definition of "income."

Now, ten years later, people have gotten what they always wanted: lower inflation and lower tax rates. Want to hear the bad news? No, I can see that you—and they—already know the bad news.

Meanwhile, the stock market—that howling, boiling cauldron of everything the folks define as "risky"—turned in an average total return over the last ten years of more than 17%. What was the ultimate "risk" in stocks over this decade? Yup, not owning them.

The Need To Define

All these factors, taken together, suggest that perhaps we ought to take about a third of the energy we now spend "selling" (or "counseling") and put it into "defining." Because, in the end, it won't matter how well you sold if the prospect literally couldn't hear you because you and he defined your terms in totally different ways.

When you get good at this, you can completely turn a sales interview around and totally recapture the agenda, just by refusing to buy into the prospect's definitions. A little courage, some elementary presence of mind, and a bit of practice are all you need. Here are some examples.

The "Risk" Of The Stock Market

Prospect: "I won't buy a stock fund. Too risky."

Superstar: "Are you referring to the short-term risk or the long-term risk?" (Silence.)

Prospect: (When he stops spluttering) "What? What the heck is the difference?"

Superstar: (With magisterial calm) "Gosh, there's the difference of night and day. Short-term stock price movements are utterly random, because the market's so inefficient in the short run. Long-term, the market's wonderfully efficient. That's because long-term, stocks reflect what the companies are doing, and great companies like Merck, Pepsi and The Gap do beautifully. The result is that, long-term, the real "risk" of the market is not owning it. Can you see what I mean?"

Low Interest Rates

Prospect: "Can't buy a bond fund now. Interest rates are too low."

Superstar: "Do you mean short-term interest rates or long-term interest rates?" (Silence.)

Prospect: "I mean interest rates!"

Superstar: "Then I think there's an opportunity here you may be missing. You see, while short-term interest rates are at 30-year lows, once you get out to 5- to 7-year rates, they're still quite wonderful... especially compared to inflation. Since you're a long-term investor, I like the Gronsky Intermediate-Term Bond Fund for you..."

Guarantee

Prospect: "Gotta keep my money in the bank. I need the guarantee."

Superstar: "Let's just make sure we understand the nature of that guarantee, to see if there's a better way to get it. Now, when your money's in the bank, who's giving you a guarantee?"

Prospect: (Proudly) "The U.S. Government!"

Superstar: "Bingo. So what does the bank do for you? Nothing, except take a cut of your interest income. Why not lend directly to the Treasury, keep all your interest, and get the guarantee directly from the source?" (This launches into a presentation of Gronsky Government Securities Fund.)

Safety

Prospect: "No stock funds. Gotta keep my money safe."

Superstar: "Help me out a little. Tell me how you define safety."

Prospect: "Why, I'm safe if I can't lose my money!"

Superstar: (Apologetically) "Forgive me; I'm still confused. Are you worried about losing the number of paper dollars you have or losing what they can buy?"

Prospect: "Now you've got *me* confused!"

Superstar: (Takes out a $100 bill.) "I've got $100 right here, clutched in my hand. If I sit here for a year, not doing anything, I'll keep it safe. Trouble is, next year at this time it'll only be worth $96. Less the next year, even less the year after that. Why, if I'd gone out on the porch with my $100 bill in 1972 and just sat there rocking, I'd still have my $100 bill...and it'd be worth about $30! Is that what you'd call safe?" (When goggle-eyed prospect shakes his head no, superstar presents Gronsky Equity Income Fund.)

* * *

Please, start redefining for your clients today. If you don't, and the stock and bond markets do half as well in the next ten years as they have in the last ten, these folks may all go bankrupt.

Sell Better By Setting Your Own Agenda

*I believe that most statements by clients and prospects which we were taught to regard as **objections** are nothing of the kind. Rather, they are attempts by the investor **to re-set the agenda in unhelpful ways.***

*Thus, when I recommend becoming a patient, long-term shareholder of the great companies in America, a prospect may say, "Stocks are too risky." I set the agenda in terms of "great companies," a term which has very favorable connotations. He didn't so much object as try to **re-set the agenda** in terms of "stocks," a term which has (at least for him) a negative connotation.*

This is very important, because all my years tell me that, in a conversation of a sales/ decision-making nature,

THE LAST PERSON WHO RE-SETS THE AGENDA WINS.

When a prospect says, "bear market," I always re-set the agenda with the phrase "big sale," as you'll see in this article.

Try it. You'll like it.

Sell Better By Setting Your Own Agenda

I'm convinced that all sales and counseling interviews we have with our clients and prospects end up following somebody's agenda: either ours or theirs.

No matter how spontaneous and intellectual these conversations appear to be at the surface, deep down we and the client have very clear and diametrically opposed agendas. At the top of our agenda is getting the client to make the wonderful investment, or to implement the terrific plan we're presenting. At the top of the client's agenda, whether he realizes it consciously or not, is getting out of having to make a decision.

Understand this: The client may not be rejecting your investment or your plan at all. He's simply trying to create a set of circumstances under which he doesn't have to make a decision. And the better you're doing your job, the more predictable this reaction is.

Why? The better we do our jobs, the more we have to try to get the client to do the opposite of whatever he wants to do at the moment. We know from bitter experience that the more our clients are convinced that some course of action is desirable (e.g., at the moment, avoiding real estate like the plague), the more profitable it will be if they take the opposite tack. And the client's deep emotional need to zig when he should zag is, in many ways, the essential conundrum of our business.

Avoiding The Bear Trap

The best way to keep your foot out of the bear trap of the client's agenda is to refuse to accept his definitions. Because again, all your experience tells you that he is usually not defining the issues in an especially useful way.

But it takes a certain kind of courage to resist your client's definition of the issues, or at least to avoid arguing with him. And that courage has to originate in the depth of your conviction. I've found that when I believe, I am believed by the people I'm talking to. Not because I know so much more than they do, but because I define the issues in completely different ways. Let me give you a f'rinstance.

Although it is already beginning to fade from memory (interestingly enough), October 19, 1987 is a classic example of something from which your client probably draws the wrong inference. And which he will, therefore, introduce into a conversation about equity mutual funds in a distinctly unhelpful way.

A risk-averse investor will almost invariably use October '87 to demonstrate what *he* means by "the risk of the stock market." The amateur in our profession will respond that, although that was indeed a terrible time, if you held on long-term you ended up OK. Which is a lot like saying that if you were on the Titanic and just treaded water for ten or twelve hours, you got rescued.

The professional, always working from his own agenda, knows that before he goes any further, he has to break up the client's definition of October 19 and replace it with a new one. But, above all, he knows he must not argue. Here's what he might say:

Client: "Oh yeah? If equities are so great, what about October 19, 1987?"

Superstar (wistfully): "Yes, it was a wonderful day. I doubt we'll get another opportunity like that in this century." (Silence.)

This reaction gives the client a megadose of cognitive dissonance: He knows exactly what he heard the superstar say, but he quite literally cannot believe he heard it. The superstar has completely regained control of the agenda, lock, stock and barrel, simply by turning the client's definition on its head.

Note that the superstar characterized October 19 as a "wonderful opportunity." He doesn't in the least accept the client's definition and then say, "Yes, but...," the way the amateur does. "Yes, but..." always ends in the death of the sales interview. The superstar, knowing that, used the opportunity to signal his client that (1) he, the superstar, has a completely unique vision of October 19 and (2) until further notice, it is his vision which will be the subject of discussion.

Client (already backing away from his definition): "I don't see how you can say October 19 was wonderful."

Superstar (intrigued, but clearly mystified): "What else would you call it? Essentially, it was a one-day, 25%-off sale on the great companies in America. And if you blinked, you missed it. Why, Gronsky Growth Fund has more than doubled since that day. Do you see why I look at it as a great opportunity?"

Client (now totally on the defensive): "But what if you had to sell?"

Superstar: "Why would you have to sell? In a properly balanced portfolio, you never have to sell, because you never have too many eggs in one basket. And besides, when you're lucky enough to get a one-day, 25%-off sale, you don't sell; you buy."

Client: "But, but...I know a lot of people who sold that day, and lost money."

Superstar (shaking his head sadly): "They were *very* badly advised." (Silence.)

The superstar, in his own serene way, is subliminally, but very effectively, communicating a couple of critically important truths here. First, that long-term, "the risk of the market" isn't in the market, it's in the investor's emotions. And second, that quality advice, of the kind the superstar is offering, is precisely what the investor needs to keep him safe from his own emotions.

Could the superstar actually say either of these things, straight out? Maybe, but I think it would be pretty tough. And you have to wonder what context he'd say them in.

And yet, in the process of totally re-setting the agenda, he's been able to imply those truths with perfect clarity. And he's done so in a way that couldn't have happened if he'd elected to argue the client's perception directly.

Another Client Gambit

Another classic way clients try to postpone the need to make a decision is to seize upon something—anything at all—which the investment you're presenting is *not*.

So, for instance, a great growth fund which owns classic blue-chip growth companies, like Pepsi, Merck and General Electric, rarely yields much more than 3%. Desperate to avoid the decision to buy some of this fund, the client will fix on the current yield. (With short rates as low as they are now, this argument is shakier than it's been in a while, but it's always there.)

Client: "The yield is less than 3%!"

Superstar (with great enthusiasm): "Exactly! That's how you know your total return is going to be so wonderful. And that your income is going to rise sharply over the years." (Superstar beams at his client, in silence.)

The amateur will dig himself into the ground trying to explain intellectually that growth companies plow most of their earnings into growing the business, rather than paying out current dividends. This is certainly true, but not useful, given what you intuitively know about the way this client thinks. First, this person has long since lost sight of the fact that stocks are companies. And second, like most risk-averse investors today, he thinks stocks mostly grow south, so the "growth" argument whizzes right past his head.

The superstar stays enthusiastically rooted in his own agenda, which contains the inexorable truth: low current yield equals high total return. But to find out what he means, the client will now have to ask a question. And in the act of doing so, the client cedes the agenda back to its rightful owner: the imperturbable professional you've always wanted to be. And will be...when you set the agenda.

Selling Through The Malaise Du Jour

What if the prospect isn't really trying to show that the investment you want him to buy won't work? **What if he's just trying to get out of having to make a decision?** What if **that's** his (hidden) agenda?

This is a question asked in the last column, and explored further in this one. I suggested that all "current events" objections are proxies for the numbing, paralyzing, nameless Fear of Making The Big Mistake.

This column introduced the technique I call VENTILATE AND VALIDATE.

Let the client **ventilate** his proxy concern. Don't argue with it; let him get it all out. Then **validate** his concern, by acknowledging that most people share that concern.

But then you make, in effect, the following lovely, non-argumentative syllogism.

(A) MOST FOLKS ARE WORRIED ABOUT (FILL IN THE BLANK: THE DEFICIT, SADDAM, WATERGATE, OPEC, HITLER/MUSSOLINI/TOJO...)

(B) IF MOST PEOPLE WERE RIGHT, MOST PEOPLE WOULD BE RICH. SINCE MOST PEOPLE SURE AIN'T RICH, IT JUST STANDS TO REASON THAT

(C) THE MALAISE DU JOUR IS A NON-STARTER **PRECISELY BECAUSE** MOST PEOPLE ARE SO WORRIED ABOUT IT.

Then, this column shows you how to do some basic therapy, trying to get behind the headlines to the nameless dread that's the real issue.

Oh, and speaking of high-button shoes: note that the deficit was the universal malaise/apocalypse du jour just two years ago. As 1995 dawns, it's dropping like a stone.

As how could it not? Because, when this column was written, **everybody** was worried about it...

Selling Through The Malaise Du Jour

In a recent column, I suggested that when prospects and clients appear to be arguing with you and resisting the investment or plan you're proposing, what they're really doing—not always, but frequently—is trying to create a situation in which they can get out of having to make a decision.

Pierpont Morgan used to warn his partners about this phenomenon by telling them, "A man always has two reasons for the things that he does: a good one, and the real one." With our clients, we usually find that the "good one" is sort of intellectual; it will often be a reference to some currently prevailing economic or political bugaboo. I call it the "malaise du jour."

But the "real one" is always emotional. I think this is something we learn very early in our careers, but somehow forget whenever the client expresses some current-events-oriented objection. All our experience tells us that the individual investor makes his financial decisions in his emotions, and then he justifies what he's done—or hasn't done—with his intellect.

Clients Dress Up Their Concerns

Real clients just don't say things like, "I'm just scared. I don't understand what's going on. I'm so afraid that I'll invest at the wrong time and end up looking like a fool." In fact, the newer your relationship with clients or prospects, and the less time you've had to infuse a healthy dose of trust into the relationship, the less likely they are to show you the raw, emotional nature of their concerns. Instead, they'll dress up those concerns in the malaise du jour.

Client: "The deficit's raging out of control; the wheels are really going to come off this time; I'm staying in cash."

or

Prospect: "Your plan sounds OK, but I wouldn't think of implementing any major changes until after the election."

Our instinctive reaction is to wrangle intellectually with the stated objection, which is the equivalent of boxing with a gigantic marshmallow. It gives where you hit, but somehow you never win.

But if you sit back and realize that the *stated* objection is merely the intellectual new clothes that the *real* naked emperor (fear) is wearing today...there's a chance you can work through it.

Avoid Wrangling With Clients

A subset of this issue is the unspoken emotional conviction in the back of everyone's mind that says: I don't ever have to buy anything from someone who's arguing with me. So, if your prospect can get you to argue that the wheels are *not* coming off, and that the deficit is *not* a terminal disease, he has gotten you to give him an excuse to end the conversation...no matter how powerful and convincing your intellectual argument is.

Instead of wrangling unproductively, try working toward a question of your own, in such a way that you soften the force of the objection while re-setting the agenda in your own terms. Let your prospect *ventilate* his concerns, make sure that you *validate* those concerns before answering...and then turn the question around on him. Here's how:

Superstar: "Yes, that's a very valid concern. I'd say that most of my clients today are worried about (the deficit) (the election). It's all you see in the newspapers and on TV these days.

"I guess my problem is exactly that. I've learned from bitter experience that when *most* folks are really worried about something, as they are today about (malaise du jour), either the problem is about to evaporate...or the exact opposite is about to happen." (silence)

Prospect: "Huh? What? When did *that* ever happen?"

Superstar: "Well, a whole bunch of times, but the last time was at the end of 1990/beginning of 1991. We'd given Saddam an ultimatum: Get out of Kuwait before January 15, or we're coming in shooting. But he didn't go anywhere.

"So *most* folks—heck, nearly everybody I talked to—said that when the shooting started, the equity market would crater, oil would soar, and that'd push inflation and interest rates sky high.

"The war broke out, right on schedule. Oil had its biggest one-day price break of all time, inflation cratered, bonds soared, and the DJIA went up 700 points without leaving a skid mark.

"That's my problem with the consensus. In the back of my mind, I keep remembering: the consensus, by definition, is the opinion of *most folks*. And if most folks were right, most folks would be rich.

"Since most folks sure aren't rich…well, I think you see where I'm going." (silence)

Now, please observe: The superstar never said—never even hinted—that the prospect was wrong. He just said: Most folks feel like you do, and this sure looks like a big problem today. But if most folks were right…

He hasn't tried to talk the prospect into, or out of, anything. He's said that *he's* learned from bitter experience, that *he* really struggles with consensus thinking, but in the back of *his* mind…

The superstar is simply sharing with the prospect some insight into how his mind works, and how diligently he tries to think through his clients' fears and concerns. Subliminally, he's beaming at the prospect what I think all real professionals project. Namely, that their primary purpose isn't so much to sell the prospect something, but to *save the prospect from himself*. And now the superstar totally regains control of the agenda by asking a question of his own.

Superstar: "But tell me, can you remember the last time you were as worried about (the economy) (the political situation) as you are now? I mean, the last time you really thought the wheels were coming off, *exactly what was going on?*"

Exploring A Client's "Real Fears"

What does the superstar think will cure the deficit? Who does he think will win the election? Who cares? The issue here is the nature of the prospect's real fears, which can only come to the surface when the prospect is talking. You can't get him talking by *telling* him anything, but you can by asking him a question.

The prospect can only come back with one of three possible answers:

1. "I've never been this worried."

2. "I'm always this worried."

3. "The last time was ('malaise d'hier.' That's French for 'yesterday's malaise')."

Here's how the superstar might handle each:

1. Never been this worried.

Superstar: "Do you think that might just be because you're getting closer to retirement and starting to worry that you'll have enough to live on? Because that's a different—and even more valid—kind of concern.

"I don't know (how the deficit's going to get cured) (who's going to win the election). But do you remember double-digit inflation? That was a real son-of-a-gun of an economic crisis, and it looked for a while as if it was here to stay. Now, it's like sideburns and bell-bottoms—a memory of a past era. (Or, if the issue is the election: "Was anybody in this century ever as poorly prepared for the presidency as Harry Truman? And now we wish we had him back.") Things in America have a funny way of turning out for the best, often in ways you least expect. Haven't you always found that?"

2. Always been this worried.

Superstar: "It's only natural, I guess. Our whole lives have to be lived in the future, and we don't know what's there, so we worry. But so often we find that tomorrow's solutions are in the actions we take today, and that, in the long run, the optimists always turn out to be the realists.

"Somebody who buried his money in a CD ten years ago has seen his income decline 75%, while somebody who bought even a so-so blue chip stock fund has seen his investment quadruple. Do you see what I mean?"

3. "Malaise d'hier"

Prospect: "You know, now that you mention it, I really used to be worried about the trade deficit, back in the mid-'80s. People said Japan was going to own everything, and we were going to be importing everything and exporting zip. Seems like just yesterday."

Superstar: "Exactly. Now the U.S. is the number one export power in the world. The Japanese stock market's down 60%, and they can't pay the mortgage on Rockefeller Center. And, with the dollar coming down, our balance of trade gets better all the time. Today, it's cheaper for a German family in Frankfurt to go to Disney World in Orlando than to Euro Disney in France. A pair of Levi's 501 jeans that costs $30 in Chicago costs about $80 in England, France and Italy.

"The budget deficit is today's problem, but tomorrow it'll be a memory...and we'll have a new problem.

"What really matters is your retirement, 12 years from now. And the question is, over those 12 years, will this investment/financial plan get you there? I believe it will. How about you?"

The keys to working through the malaise du jour, then, are: empathy, avoiding argument at all costs, solving for the real personal worry rather than the six o'clock news version, and relating back to yesterday's evanescent crises.

Intellectual facts are fine, but emotional truth will carry the day every time.

Are You Selling The Serum Or The Snakes?

*Come to think of it, the first time I really noticed a lot of people talking to me about my column rather than about **Serious Money** was when "Serum or the Snakes" came out. People loved it. And, now that I've re-read it, so do I, all over again.*

*I've often tried to make the point that nobody ever bought a mutual fund (or an encyclopedia, or a set of pots and pans) because of **what it is.** People only buy something because of what they perceive that **it will do for them.** This column is the best analogy for that phenomenon I've yet come up with: the snakes are **what it is;** the serum is **what it does for you.***

*This article also marked a significant advance beyond **Serious Money**. The book states Murray's Great Law of Presentations: The quality of a money management presentation is an inverse function of its length. In this piece, I offered a corollary, or Second Law:*

"THE QUALITY OF A PRESENTATION IS AN INVERSE FUNCTION OF THE NUMBER OF NUMBERS IN IT."

Are You Selling The Serum Or The Snakes?

My best pal, Indiana Jones, has (unbeknownst to him) contracted a rare disease on one of his expeditions to a tropical jungle. He'll be dead in a year, unless he takes a serum made from the venom of a particularly vicious species of snake.

So, with my buddy's best interests uppermost in my mind and heart, I go out and collect a whole bunch of these snakes and take 'em over to Indy's house in a burlap bag. I toss the writhing, hissing bag of snakes on Indy's kitchen table and start explaining the situation to him.

In the middle of my very first sentence, I hear the kitchen door slam, and when I look up, Indiana is long gone. How could I have forgotten: he hates snakes!

The threat of slow death months and months from now was nowhere near frightening enough to keep him in the same room with those snakes. And given what I clearly know about his irrational fears, I should have anticipated that.

I just as easily could have stopped off at a laboratory, had the guys in the white coats extract the venom from the snakes' fangs, cook up the serum, and give it to Indy, mixed in with his favorite soft drink.

But no, not me. I had to prove what a hero I am. I had to force Indy to sit through a presentation of my Herculean effort in getting the bag of snakes. The result: instant and total failure. Indy still doesn't see what a neat thing I did for him...and he's still dying.

What's The Message

This parable is not too far removed from what many of us are doing in our efforts to sell equity mutual funds to risk-averse investors—those millions of Americans who are slowly dying of the disease called extinction of your purchasing power.

I think our problem arises from the fact that we use exactly the same presentation with people who know and like equity funds as we do with people who hate and fear stocks. The bag-of-snakes approach works fine with a guy who says, "Snakes, mice, wombats, whatever: just tell me what I have to do so I don't die!" But with Indy, it was worse than a waste of time; it was counterproductive, because now I don't even know where he went.

Since the overriding truth of equity investing is that success is about time, and not about timing, you know that all a client has to do is get comfortable and stay comfortable. Ride it out long-term (dollar-cost averaging along the way, if you can) and you're always a winner, relative to so-called "safe" debt instruments. With the risk-averse investor, you're always selling comfort...or you're not selling at all. And comfort is always built on trust, not on facts.

Nothing that I said to Indiana about that bag of snakes was wrong—but he was in no emotional shape to accept it the way I presented it to him. And I had every reason to know that. I blew it.

Here's a pertinent example of snakes vs. serum in everyday life:

Snakes: "This fund earns Morningstar's 5-star rating."

Serum: "This portfolio is managed by Grey Trueheart. He's 58 years old, and he's been managing clients' portfolios for nearly 30 years. He's very cautious, but he always seems to produce very good long-term returns. He spoke at a dinner I attended in Boston last month, and he said..."

Make Your Client Comfortable

Look at all the comforting, subliminal messages packed into the Grey Truehart/Serum statement.

1. The manager is a real flesh-and-blood professional. I know his name; I know how long he's been in this business.

2. I understand his style: cautious (risk-averse investors love that), but he performs over time. How do I denominate performance? If the investor wants to know that, let him ask me. Maybe he doesn't care, as long as *I'm* comfortable ("Snakes, mice, whatever...").

(Note: In my book *Serious Money*, I postulated Murray's Great Law of Presentations, to wit: **The quality of a money management presentation is an inverse function of its length.** Let me now offer Murray's Second Law of Presentations: **The quality of a presentation is an inverse function of the number of numbers in it.** Statistics—especially performance statistics—may often be intellectual facts, but they rarely contribute to emotional truth. And the prospect always makes his investment decisions in his emotions, not in his intellect.)

3. I had dinner with the guy. (Murray's Third Law: one piece of bread, broken with the manager, is the emotional equivalent of nine statistics.) I know how he's thinking. I'm comfortable with how he's thinking. OK? (If not OK; talk to me. Tell me where it hurts. Let me make you feel better. NOT: Let me make you the recipient of six more empty facts which your head refuses to process because your tummy hurts.)

The Data Approach

Now let's look at the wonderfulness of the responses to the dizzying data onslaught/Snakes variation. (Don't misunderstand my point, firms such as Morningstar and CDA/Weisenberger do an excellent job of analyzing mutual funds. But some clients panic when someone starts spewing forth data from a source they've never even heard of.)

What might a client as afraid of stocks as Indy is of snakes say if you hit him between the eyes with a data deluge? Here are five possibilities—none of them too pleasant.

1. What's a Morningstar? Wait, now I remember; it was a movie with Natalie Wood. She's dead now. If I buy this fund, will I be dead, too?

2. Five stars out of how many? Four? Nine? A hundred and nine? So what? Who cares?

3. I don't know what any of that means. You've reminded me how abysmally ignorant I am about mutual funds. My tummy hurts. I'm just gonna roll over my CD.

4. Who's Mr. Morningstar? What makes him an expert? My brother-in-law lost money in a stock fund. Does that make him an expert?

5. Five stars when the market's up for ten years. How many stars when the market tanks, like it's gonna do (next week, next year, next St. Swithin's Day)?

More Snakes And Serum Side-By-Side

Here are two more examples of raw data vs. pasteurized truth. Note that they both say the very same thing.

Snakes: "Since its founding in 1924, the fund has produced an average annual total return, counting reinvested dividends and assuming you paid the taxes from another source, of 11.7% vs. 10.4% for the S&P 500."

Serum: "If your father or grandfather just put $10,000 in this portfolio the day they started it up in 1924, and just left it alone…well, if you're still working today, it's because you want to, not because you have to."

Now, observe the complete opposite client reactions that these two styles provoke:

Snake: In 70 years, they couldn't beat the market by more than one percent? And for this you want me to pay a 4 1/2% load? Yuck.

Serum: The American Dream. My forebears invested patiently, wisely…and my family is rich now. Hey, I love this. If my grandson is rich because of something I do today, maybe he'll never forget me, and in that sense, I'll never die. Gee…

The Bottom Line

I think you see what I mean. To find out where you stand on the Serum/Snake scale, I suggest you record your favorite presentation today. Then take a yellow legal pad and make two columns: "Snakes" and "Serum."

Now play the tape back. For each sentence that's a dose of serum, make a check mark under "Serum"; same for "Snakes." If you don't have three check marks under "Serum" for every one check mark under "Snakes," you're in real trouble.

Even better, do this with a colleague. Make your column headings, then make your presentations to each other. And score each other's presentation with check marks.

This may not be the most fun you've ever had, but it'll tell you very quickly whether you're nurturing your client's trust...or punishing him for his fears.

Why Aren't You More Bullish?

Once again, I saw the new year as very, very bullish. I particularly thought most people were missing the implications of the huge middle-class "tax cut" implicit in the home refinancing boom. I marveled at—and loved—how low consumer confidence remained. Indeed, my favorite line from this piece is:

*"CONFIDENCE IS A LAGGING INDICATOR; IT COMES BACK **AFTER** THE FUNDAMENTALS HAVE STRAIGHTENED THEMSELVES OUT, NOT BEFORE!"*

The year 1993 would, I believed, be "a sad, bad time to be a bear," and so it was...until right near the end.

Why Aren't You More Bullish?

It's been my experience that our clients end up with the same attitudes toward the future that we have—that's why they stay our clients. So, if you're having trouble getting clients to invest with confidence right now, maybe you ought to take a look at your own convictions—or the absence thereof—concerning this next block of time. Because it isn't fair, or even good psychology, to expect folks to be more confident about the future than you are.

Confidence, however, is mighty hard to come by these days. And you may be feeling that absence of confidence very keenly. So this is an important time to remember a couple of things about confidence. First, confidence is a lagging indicator; it comes back after the fundamentals have straightened themselves out, not before. Second, in a very real way, the presence or absence of confidence is also a perverse indicator.

When everybody is very effervescent and unworried, they tend to be pretty fully invested. So who's left to buy? And if there's nobody left to buy, markets have a tough time going up. If, on the other hand, confidence is extraordinarily low—as it certainly is now—there's usually a lot of profit to be made, as all of that money sitting on the sidelines (someday) pours back into the market.

Taking Stock Of The Positives

Becoming more confident about the future usually requires some hard facts. So here are nine things to reflect on as you gear up for your 1993 sales push.

• **Consumer Confidence**—The most widely watched index of consumer confidence (whose baseline is 100) was established in 1985. Recently, that index plummeted to 53. If you accept the index's validity, you're stuck with the conclusion that folks are only half as confident regarding the future today as they were seven years ago. Forgive me, but that's wildly, howlingly bullish.

• **Economic Recovery**—It's been very popular, these last few quarters, to decry the painfully slow U.S. economic recovery—with GNP growing at not much better than a 1.5% annual rate. This analysis ignores a couple of important things, however. First, the economy is growing, not declining. Second, though it's perfectly true that the consumer hasn't been consuming, take a look at what he has been doing: paying down debt like there's no tomorrow.

In the '80s debt orgy, consumers ran up their monthly credit obligations to a record 17.5% of their income. After this big, bad, long recession, they really got spooked, and they've whittled that number down to 14.5%, today. Which, incidentally, is about where it usually bottoms, as consumers feel comfortable starting to spend again. And each one-point drop in this figure unleashes about $40 billion—yes, billion dollars—of potential purchasing power.

• **Mortgage Rates**—If you haven't already, you might focus for a moment on the powerful potential effects of the precipitous drop in home mortgage rates. When folks can recast their 11% to 13% home loans at 8.5%, they do it. Hundreds of thousands of us have refinanced our mortgages and are now looking at several hundred dollars a month in incremental cash flow.

And sooner or later, we'll do one of two things: start spending that extra money (in which case the economy will boom) or invest it (in which case the economy will boom). (This effect is even more pronounced in Canada, America's largest trading partner; home loan rates there have halved.) It's the equivalent of a massive middle-class tax cut...which is, of course, profoundly stimulative.

• **Inflation**—Speaking of effective "tax cuts," inflation dropping from 5% to 2% has much the same positive effect on household budgets as does the cratering of energy costs, which in real terms are back where they were in 1974! And you wonder why total vehicle sales (including cars and light trucks) in early November were up 16.5% year-over-year? And department store sales were ahead 7.5%?

• **Exports**—Remember, too, that the U.S. is now the largest exporting nation in the world (having doubled its exports in just the last five years) and that our major trading partners—Japan and Europe—are in deep recession. The next major move in those economies is up (though it may take a while longer), and when that happens, U.S. exports will boom.

• **Productivity**—Meanwhile, we're getting more productive every day. Manufacturing productivity rose 2.4% over the last four quarters. That, plus declining wage inflation, means manufacturing unit labor costs have actually fallen 0.2% in the last year. As a global competitor, then, we've literally never been in better shape.

• **Fiscal Problems**—Because bad news is good copy, you get a lot of information from journalists about our fiscal problems (translation: the deficit). But it is insufficiently noted that our monetary performance in the last ten years is one of the great economic triumphs of the age. With gold in the $230s and the CRB futures index languishing around 200, inflation's under better control than it's been since the 1950s.

• **Corporate Profits**—All of that means higher corporate profits—the ultimate leading indicator of economic activity ahead. Earnings of non-financial companies have risen $50 billion—a whopping 14%—since 3Q91. The S&P 500's earnings were up about 30% in the third quarter compared to last year—and would have been up over 40% if not for the hugely negative effect of IBM. No wonder, then, that new claims for unemployment benefits were hitting two-year lows by mid-November.

• **Interest Rates**—Had interest rates started ticking up a little by Thanksgiving? Sure they had—just exactly the way you'd expect them to when a broad, deep, powerful economic recovery really gets up a head of steam. Speaking of upticks, have you noticed what's been happening to small-cap stocks lately, as reflected in the near-record highs for the NASDAQ index?

The Bottom Line

Fellas and gals, here's some friendly advice: get your head out of today. Over this next year, the first post-Cold War global economic recovery will start to unfold. The U.S. is already there, Canada's on the cusp, Japan and Europe will start to turn later on in '93. This next block of time is probably going to be a sad, bad time to be a bear...particularly if our clients get left behind because of our timidity.

Our clients are getting just about enough management—that's what the mutual fund/variable annuity/wrap-fee sales explosion is all about. What they're crying for is more leadership. Let's resolve to give it to them in the new year.

If not us, who? If not now…when?

Conquering Prospects' Fear With Four Questions

(And Two Postage Stamps)

*This was the most widely reprinted of these columns, up until that time. People really seemed to like the four-questions script, and especially the postage stamp idea (which I'd actually been using for some time, and which was in **Serious Money**).*

*But the real point of this article was that we were going about the task of selling to the so-called risk-averse investor all wrong. Our training—the classic transaction-oriented sales skills of reason and argument—was premised on the client's problem being **ignorance**. I said it's **fear**. And the first thing you learn as an adult about fear is that you **can't** reason with it:*

*"THE ANTIDOTE FOR FEAR ISN'T INFORMATION, IT'S **TRUST**."*

*Though the golden moment of 3% short rates is long over, the basic premise of the column seems to me more true than ever. It is that savers immolate themselves on the altar of stability of principal, never seeing that, net of inflation and taxes, they're being destroyed. (You can—and should—save for the down payment on a house. But you can't "save" for retirement, you have to **invest** for it.) The stamps are the best way I've ever found to make this point without arguing. People have told me, for my whole career, that the prices of stocks were going to go down. **But no one has ever told me that the price of a stamp was going to go down.**

Conquering Prospects' Fear With Four Questions
(And Two Postage Stamps)

Despite the fact that they're earning a blended rate of under 3%, millions of your fellow Americans have nearly $4 trillion of their household financial assets (out of about $15.4 trillion in total) languishing in "three black holes:" money market funds, bank CDs and short-term Treasuries.

The overwhelming majority of that money is held by two classes of people: (1) Americans with a clear personal memory of the Depression, and (2) their children. The latter group (those born between, say, 1938 and 1950) may be too young to remember the horror of the Depression. But their attitudes toward money and risk come from parents who lived through (and never got over) those terrible years. Which explains why you keep running into 45-year-olds with all their money in fixed-income investments. Though born in 1947, the year stocks began the great 22-year post-war bull market, these investors aren't working off their life experiences. They're working off their parents' Depression-ravaged unconscious.

The Depression taught people that there was only one economic good—preservation of principal *as an end in itself*. By this logic, there exists only one risk: losing your money. Which, in the absence of some "guarantee," these folks regard not just as a risk but as a virtual certainty. ("If stocks *can* go down, then they *will* go down...and they'll *never come back.*")

Trouble is, the Depression was a complete and total anomaly: a relatively brief, though acutely horrific, moment of deflation in a world of permanent decline in purchasing power (a/k/a inflation). And if you get your definitions from an anomaly—as the owners of the $4 trillion most assuredly did—then your resulting investment decisions aren't just wrong. They're 180 degrees around from right.

Focusing On The Overwhelming Risk

As I suggested in this space back in August ("Stop Selling, Start Redefining"), capital loss, while it'll always be *a* risk, can never again be *the* risk. The overwhelming financial risk in American life today is extinction of our purchasing power: the chance that we'll outlive our income, then outlive our principal, and still not be even remotely dead.

Our principal has no intrinsic value, in other words. It's only worth the purchasing power of the income stream it produces. This is a total abstraction to the children of deflation, to whom principal is a sacred thing. And, in order to perserve principal, these folks continue to make only investments that, net of inflation and taxes, usually return zero or less.

Thus, in a world of constantly rising costs of living, the children of deflation invest so that their purchasing power is constantly being sandpapered away. They call their mode of investing "safe;" I call it suicide. In a rising-cost world, investing for capital preservation alone (at the expense of purchasing power) is the ultimate recklessness.

You know that; I know that; Ibbotson knows that. So how come the holders of that $4 trillion stay out there in the dark and cold? One big reason, I think, is the way we sell.

The Antidote For Fear

If you listen to yourself sell (or counsel) all day today, you'll find that you're constantly purveying one or more of four things: reason, facts, numbers and/or proof. (The Ibbotson chart, being the apotheosis of all four of these attributes, is our industry's Centerfold-of-the-Millennium. And we can't figure out why it makes the so-called risk-averse investor's eyes glaze over.)

Trouble is, the issues standing between us and the nice people who hold the $4 trillion aren't susceptible to intellectual argument. If they were, the Ibbotson chart would immediately convince everybody. Since it convinces almost nobody, I think we can safely conclude that the problem here isn't intellectual (i.e. ignorance); it's emotional (i.e. FEAR).

And the antidote for fear isn't information, it's *trust.* That's a totally different (and, I believe, antithetical) kind of sale. Hiding behind pieces of paper like the Ibbotson chart sends the client exactly the wrong message. It says, in effect, you don't have to trust me, because I can *prove* my argument. But no proof can mitigate fear. Your brain may be wired for AC, but the prospect's heart is a DC appliance.

The Four Questions

So here's what I suggest. Go see your prospect. (Don't try to do this work over the phone. The phone is a medium for the exchange of information; face-to-face is the medium for the exchange of trust.) Then, don't tell him anything; *ask him stuff.*

This advice is based on my belief that, in any sales/counseling interview, the party who asks the most questions always wins. Conversely, the party who makes the largest number of statements loses. Non-salespeople (and poor salespeople) seem to think the great salesperson is a great talker. But, in my experience, he/she is a great *questioner*, probing always for the prospect's greatest fears.

At this golden moment, when 3% short rates are driving the so-called risk-averse investor nearly mad (I invested only in "safe" investments; why are my financial goals fading into the mist?), try these four questions on him and see what happens.

1. Are your investments producing an adequate return *for you?*

Stress the last two words; I'm probing his viscera, not asking his opinion.

Now observe: I could have said, "Your investments aren't producing an adequate return for you." He'd have snapped, "Maybe not, but at least I can't lose my money." And in five seconds, we'd have completed the sequence Statement-Argument-Endgame. Instead, I ask him the question (to which I already know the answer). And when he says, "No, they sure aren't"—with pain and anger—I've started to mine the discontent that's essential to all major sales.

Incidentally, if you don't think that the universal "No" answer to this question is a big deal, cast your mind back to 1981. Then, the client owned a 15% money fund, a 15.77% six-month CD, and a 16% two-year Treasury note. Asked the same question, he'd have grinned and asked, "You *bet* they are, sonny, now what's on your mind?" A mighty shaky platform from which to launch a major sales presentation, don't you think?

Now, the second question.

2. Are your investments getting you closer to, or further away from, your lifetime financial goals?

This is a big discomfort generator. Yes, his principal is "safe," and so, he can sustain himself in his current state of denial on that issue. So you do an end-around, sending the question deep into the emotional backfield of his fear that he's not getting closer to having enough to retire on, or to send his kids to college with. (If you got 3% on your investments this year, and Whatsamatta U. raised its tuition, room and board charges 6%, the light at the end of the tunnel just may be the headlight of an oncoming freight train.) Principal is an abstraction if your purchasing power is turning to sand—but the prospect has to arrive at that conclusion himself. You can't deliver it to him, especially if there's "nobody home" emotionally.

3. Will you tell me, please, what's the greatest financial risk you and your family face for the balance of your lifetime?

Most folks are going to be stunned at this question, and you'll have galvanized their attention even more. People are so used to thinking there's only one risk—principal loss—that this question, suggesting as it does a hierarchy of risks, may really shake them up.

When the answer comes back, "The big risk in my life is that I'll lose my money," I get to make a lot of heavy eye contact with the prospect while just shaking my head slowly from side to side. (It's another little sales technique I picked up along the way; nonverbal communication. Try it sometime.) Then I say, "That's not the risk. It's *a* risk. But it can never again, in your and my lifetime, be *the* risk. This is *the* risk."

At that point, I go into my pocket and take out a little thing I always carry. It's a small plastic stamp holder with two U.S. first-class postage stamps: one from the current year and one from 20 years earlier. I try to get stamps that are as similar as possible; that was easy this past year because there were Olympics in both 1992 and 1972. (You can get the older stamps from any good stamp dealer; I get mine from Subway Stamp Shop in New York City, 1-800-221-9960. The Post Office publishes a catalog of all its old stamps for $10, so you can choose the one you want to use.) The 1972 stamp has "8 cents" on it; the 1992 stamp, of course, says "29 cents."

I hold this set of stamps up to the prospect (for a very long time, as you'll see) as I say, "*This* is *the* risk." Then I add, "And the sooner you and I want to retire, and the longer we want to live, the greater this risk becomes." If he's already retired, I just say, "...the longer you want to live..."

Note that I don't use the word "inflation." In my experience, inflation is a complete abstraction that means 100 different things to 100 different people. To a lot of 'em, it means 1979-82, or a phenomenon that's past. So I rely on the symbols (the stamps), which are always more powerful than the word.

As an alternative to the stamps, I suppose I could have shown my prospect the line on the Ibbotson chart that delineates inflation. But that'd just make his eyes glaze over. Why? Because it's a *fact*. Facts get admitted to the prospect's *intellect*—where there's no decision making going on. The stamps are the *truth*. Truth is different from fact, and truth gets admitted to the prospect's *emotions*. Bull's-eye!

Now, with the stamps still in front of the prospect's eyes, I drop the hammer with Question Four.

4. Are your investments defending you against this risk, or are they exposing you to it?

I hear lots of different answers to this question, but they all come under the same two basic headings. One is sort of, "Oh my God!" This tells me the prospect gets the essential concept. Alternatively, I'll hear some version of, "What do you mean?" Then, for the first and last time, I'll take the stamps out of his face. I'll look at them for just a moment myself. Then I'll put them back in front of him and say, with deadly seriousness—*"I guess I mean this: If your investments were returning 8 cents in 1972, are they returning at least 29 cents today?"*

When my prospect answers that, of course, they're not, the four questions can report "mission accomplished." Because, at this golden moment of 3% short rates, I believe that if you (1) get physically in front of the prospect, (2) ask him these four questions, and (3) show him your two stamps...well, you're about 70% of the way to getting him to buy whatever investment (or plan) you present.

Battling Toxic
Definitions Syndrome

*This article is deliberately presented here out
of chronological sequence, inasmuch as it is the
sequel to "Four Questions/Two Postage Stamps."
This piece offered further scripting, based on the
premise that, when you run into an advanced
case of Toxic Definitions Syndrome, you need to
question the pathology rather than **argue** with it.*

*The phenomenon which we generally refer to
as risk-aversion is, I believe, a multigenerational
emotional disturbance: people got it from their
parents, who got it from The Great Deflation of
the 1930's. The person who looks at an asset
class (shares of the Great Companies) that went
from 40 to 4000 in 62 years—and calls that asset
class "too risky"—isn't actually risk-averse. He's
emotionally disturbed.*

*So we need to rely not on the traditional skills
of selling (reason and argument), but the skills of
a therapist, who questions why his patient feels
the way he feels. As the article says:*

> *"IT'S CENTRAL TO THE
> EMOTIONAL MAKE-UP OF ALL
> HUMAN BEINGS THAT THEY
> DON'T HAVE TO BUY ANYTHING
> FROM ANYBODY WHO
> ARGUES WITH 'EM."*

Battling Toxic Definitions Syndrome

Two months ago, I suggested using the "Four Questions and Two Postage Stamps" presentation as an antidote for Toxic Definitions Syndrome, the epidemic of financial blight that has spread through savers' and investors' portfolios in recent years.

I call this disease Toxic Definitions Syndrome because it's quite literally the client's definitions of two basic concepts—risk and safety—that are killing him. The major symptoms of this disease are (1) a portfolio hideously overweighted with fixed-income securities (particularly those at the short end of the maturity spectrum) and (2) a portfolio with a correspondingly underweighted (or non-existent) equity exposure.

This month, I want to provide more ways you can battle Toxic Definitions Syndrome, focusing primarily on the technique of **asking** rather than **telling** clients the critical truths of long-term investing.

Reviewing Basic Premises

The great mass of today's savers/investors get their definitions of risk and safety either directly from the experience of the Depression, or—one generation removed—from the Depression-ravaged attitudes of their parents.

The Depression was a massive—but momentary—deflation. And deflation is an anomaly: not just different from reality, but its opposite. The Depression taught us that both risk and safety were a function of your principal. But the real risk is purchasing power, and the only safety is the accretion of purchasing power after inflation and taxes.

Our primary goal has to be to cure these toxic definitions. But that isn't what most of us are trying to do. Instead, we're usually treating the disease's symptoms (i.e. the client's portfolio) rather than the disease itself—the definitions.

Thus, every so often, when the equity market has been going up for a while, we may have some short-term success in overcoming fear by administering the narcotic of greed. But when that drug wears off—which it tends to do suddenly—the basic disease (fear of losing principal) returns in an even-more-powerful strain.

A One-Way Ticket To Palookaville

At that point, we retreat to our two usual devices: saying "Yes, but" and/or arguing directly with the client's definitions. Both of which are a one-way ticket to Palookaville. Please observe.

• **"Yes, But…"**—Guy calls and says he has a 3% CD coming due, and he's going to roll it over unless we have something better for him to do with the money. We go racing over to his house with a beautiful, bedrock equity income fund that hasn't had a down year since '74. Guy says, "It isn't guaranteed." And we say "Yes, but…" and we feel ourselves die. Indeed, we always die when we say "Yes, but…" We finish the sentence, but it's essentially a post-mortem reflex.

Fact is, we deserve to die for saying "Yes, but…" First, we're trying to sell better returns to people who aren't primarily (or even secondarily) motivated by returns. If they were motivated by returns they wouldn't be lending out $4 trillion at 2.9%—would they?

Far more important, we deserve the oblivion which "Yes, but…" surely brings because, in the act of saying those two dreadful words, **we've accepted the client's definitions.** And, in the act of accepting his definitions, we give him permission to roll over the CD—which is what he was really looking for when he called us in the first place. You see, the money won't move until the definitions move. And the definitions won't move until you stop accepting them.

• **Direct Argument**—Guy says, "Stocks are too risky". We say, in effect if not in so many words, "No, they're not". The good news is that intellectually we're right. The bad news is that we've just ended the sales interview, by the most effective means ever devised: starting an argument.

You see, it's central to the emotional make-up of all human beings that they don't have to buy anything from anybody who argues with 'em. That's why when you hold up the Ibbotson chart in response to the objection that stocks are too risky, you always wake up three minutes later out on the sidewalk, with no conscious memory of how you got there. The Ibbotson chart is the most intellectually rigorous way we've yet found to argue, "No, they're not." And it still gets you thrown out, every single time. Because it never matters how elegant your arguments are. By arguing, you leave the toxic definitions in place.

The only right answer is, of course, a question. Once and for all: the only possible right answer to the objection "Stocks are too risky" is **"How do you define risk?"**

Well, isn't it? I mean, hasn't the client come right to the heart of the matter—his definition of risk as principal vs. your definition of risk as purchasing power? Similarly, the only answer to the objection "Can't buy your equity income fund; gotta keep my money safe," is, of course, **"How do you define safety?"**

Because, of course, this client has just confessed that he can't tell the difference between **safety** (accretion of purchasing power after inflation and taxes) and **certainty** (having somebody guarantee that he'll always have the same number of dollars—irrespective of what they'll buy). But, he hasn't heard himself confess that. And the only way to take him back to his definitions without arguing is to question those definitions.

You have to lead the discussion back to the essential truth that the ultimate risk is loss of purchasing power. And you may have to do it again and again, even within the same interview, because it's so overwhelmingly counterintuitive to most folks that they tend to keep backsliding. (I recently had two brokers swear to me that they'd made the Four Questions/Two Stamps presentation word-for-word as it appeared in the February issue. The first broker's prospect said, "OK, but what have you got that's guaranteed?" And the second's said, "That's very interesting. Now what's your current CD rate?" There's a very powerful instinct for denial at work here. It's like when the doctor says, "It's terminal," and the patient asks, "What do you mean, it's germinal?")

So, even if the client looked in horror at my two Olympic commemorative bobsled team postage stamps—the 1972 8 cent version right next to the 1992 29 cent number—he's still likely to respond to the question "How do you define risk?" with the instinctive "Losing my money!"

Thus, the stamps (and not the spoken word "inflation") have to come back out again. As Sherlock Holmes might have said of the stamps' earlier appearance, my prospect **saw** them but did not **observe** them. If he had, he wouldn't still be equating risk with principal. To stay locked on to the proper target, then, you have to keep asking yourself "Has he bought my definitions yet?" rather than "Has he bought my fund yet?"

Remember: loss of principal is a risk...a relatively low-level risk, and one that's very easy to defend against. (And remember, too, that the ultimate weapon against loss of principal is broad diversification across several asset classes, not burying your money in a black hole like a CD or a money fund.)

But loss of principal can never again in our lifetimes be **the** risk. Rather, **the** risk is that we'll outlive our money. Unfortunately, this is a terribly difficult concept for people who've believed all their lives that the only risk was loss of principal.

Framing Your Questions

When you get good at this, you'll be able to frame your questions so they lead away from the issue of principal as an end in itself, and toward an appreciation of purchasing power as the key to everything. As always, the party to a sales interview who asks the most questions wins.

Superstar: "Am I right that you're investing for the production of an income after you retire?"

Prospect: "You bet."

Superstar: "What are you going to do with that income?"

Prospect: "Huh?"

Superstar: "Picture yourself already retired. You're getting income from your investments. What do you do with it?"

Prospect: "This is either the zaniest trick question I ever heard, or the answer is: I use it to buy stuff."

Superstar: "Bingo. You'll take your income in retirement, buy everything you need, and then, if you have some money left over, you'll buy some things you just want. Now: What's the price of everything you need—and everything you want—going to do every day for the rest of your life?"

Prospect: "Go through the *!?* roof, just like it always has!"

Superstar: "Exactly! So the income you're investing to produce better be going up at the same rate, or you and your wife are going to be in a bad place, right?"

Prospect: "Gee, I guess so." (or, alternatively, "Huh?" In which case, get ready to show him the stamps again.)

Superstar: "So your real investment objective—like mine—is a retirement income that can go up at least as quickly as your costs rise?"

Prospect: "Never thought about it that way, but...well, sure."

Superstar: (Rolls right into his presentation of Gronsky Dividend Growth Fund, a portfolio of companies whose dividends have increased over the last ten years at a rate higher than the CPI.)

Once again: stop selling, start redefining. Stop telling people things; start asking 'em stuff. And don't try to treat the symptom (the portfolio) until you've cured the disease (Toxic Definitions Syndrome).

Funds To Buy In All Seasons

*A vexing problem of our profession is getting the investor to make a decision. The only thing harder is to get him to make **another** decision, in timely recognition of the need for change.*

Over the last few years, quite a number of asset allocation funds have appeared, and I devoted this column to the great conceptual strengths of this kind of fund.

*They are a great way to get people moving when neither you or the folks have any concept of where the markets are going to go next. That is, if you believe in the manager of an asset allocation fund, you believe that he'll get you (and keep you) in harmony with the major trends. Thus, **there's really no wrong time to buy a good asset allocation fund**, so you can do business without making a "call" on the markets.*

*Asset allocation funds also provide instant, broad, economical diversification. And **diversification**, acting in concert with **time**, kills the risk of principal loss. Even more important, as the article says, such a fund:*

"...FREES THE INVESTOR FROM HAVING TO WORRY ABOUT CHANGING HIS INVESTMENTS EVERY TIME THE WIND BLOWS FROM A DIFFERENT DIRECTION."

As 1995 dawned, the crosscurrents in the market seemed to me to make this column—and indeed these funds—worth another look.

Funds To Buy In All Seasons

First, the good news: With short-term rates hovering in the 3% range, you have unprecedented access to the huge pool of money still gasping for air at the short end of the yield curve.

As frightened and paralyzed as investors in CDs, money-market funds and similar types of investment vehicles may be right now, they're getting desperate to do *something*. (That's why investment advisors who specialize in doing seminars report that their audiences are running double and triple what they were a year ago.) Now, what are you going to recommend?

That's the bad news. The equity markets have soared since the 1987 Crash. And, even though the broad averages have been basically marking time for the past 12 months, they've been doing so at lofty levels, relative to earnings, dividends and book value. Small-cap, meanwhile, has gone to the moon. Even REITs have blasted into the stratosphere. A lot of us are coming down with a bad case of the "too lates." After all, what good is it to coax someone out of CDs and into a nice, easy-going equity income fund only to have the fund's NAV go into a power dive? Capturing assets is great, but retaining them is what counts.

Ditto bond funds—in fact, even more so. It's not that tough a sale to get folks to trade in their tired old CDs on a brand-spanking-new, intermediate-term corporate bond fund. But, in a strong economic recovery (which you can no longer be sure we're not having), there may be significant upward pressure on rates, particularly from these low levels.

Standing Pat Has A Downside

So you may elect to just let the old earth take a couple of turns while the markets sort themselves out. And then you'll know what to tell folks. Admirably cautious though this stance may be, it's got a couple of significant drawbacks.

First, watching and waiting doesn't usually generate much revenue. Second, while you're being studiously silent, some other salesperson/planner may come along with a Jim-dandy idea that looks to your prospect like a nifty alternative to doing nothing.

Third, and most important, the window of opportunity implicit in 3% short rates won't stay open forever. And my guess is that when there's a sign in the bank window that says "ONE-YEAR CD: 5.9%...", well, put the chairs up on the tables, turn out the lights, and the last one out please lock up. The game will be over.

Remember: You think your worst enemy is the investor's fear. But it's not. Far more deadly to your book-building efforts is investor complacency. And, after suffering 12 years of declining rates, the investor may regard even a pop to the 5 1/2% to 6% range as nirvana—particularly if inflation is half that.

Go For Diversification

My suggestion: Find a nice asset allocation fund that you can learn to love in a hurry. Because a credible asset allocation fund is not just a fund for all seasons—though it is certainly that. More important, it's a way of always being right—if, and to the extent that, the manager responds to changes in market climate in a measured, disciplined and consistent way.

The key to your ability to offer an asset allocation fund successfully is an informed belief on your part—as opposed to, say, a deep, nuanced, intellectual understanding of the truth and beauty of the Bailard, Biehl & Kaiser Diversified Portfolio Index. Remember: When you believe, you'll be believed. And the folks don't care what you know until they know that you care.

Pick a couple or three asset allocation funds. Then ask each fund's wholesaler to take you through his fund's discipline and methodology. NOTE: If the wholesaler can't explain the basic discipline in a cogent, lucid way (or if he can, but it ends up sounding like alchemy, or communication with the spirit world), take a pass. Remember Murray's Law of the Inexorable Justice of Wholesaling, which states that all money management organizations eventually end up with the wholesalers they deserve.

If the basic discipline strikes you as sensible, and the record suggests that the discipline is being consistently followed *in response to* changes in market climate, you've found your fund. I stress the phrase *in response to* change. Any wholesaler who tells you his fund can consistently *anticipate* change—who says, in other words, that his fund can time the markets—is to be avoided like the plague. Nobody can consistently time the markets. **Nobody.**

Making The Sale

You'll want to pursue this line of inquiry further with your firm's mutual fund due diligence officer. This is, after all, a sales and marketing column, so let's talk about selling asset allocation funds.

Diversification. The first great strength of an asset allocation fund—at least one that includes all three major asset classes: stocks, bonds, and cash—is that it's an instantly diversified portfolio. And broad diversification effectively kills the risk of principal loss.

Diversification doesn't get you any particular return—after all, if you homogenize out the risk, you do roughly the same to the return. But your prospects aren't primarily motivated by return. If they were, they wouldn't be lending their money at 3%, now would they? Their primary concern is with avoiding risk of principal. Diversification may sound bland to you, like apple pie or the flag, but it's a pretty big deal to these folks, once they understand what it does for them. So don't be shy about selling it pretty hard.

Freedom From Worrying About Change. By far the most important benefit of an asset allocation fund is that it frees the investor from having to worry about changing his investments every time the wind blows from a different direction.

You and I thrive on change; it makes life interesting, and it means we get to re-deploy folks' assets and earn some income thereby. So we may be reluctant to admit that, in our hearts, we know that real people loathe and despise change—and the need to make decisions—almost as much as they hate risk. And the older they get, as I've said before in this column, the more they hate it. (The $4 trillion in money markets, CDs and short Treasuries isn't there for the 3% yield. It's there for the enormous psychic income that comes from never having to make a decision.)

A credible asset allocation fund is constantly making those decisions—and those portfolio adjustments—for you. If you stress the enormous emotional relief implicit in this benefit, rather than trying to teach your prospect the methodology—which is certain death—you may really put some points on the board.

A Bulletproof Sale

As a salesman, there's something else I really like about asset allocation funds: They don't give the prospect much of a target to shoot at, in terms of questions/objections.

A typical question is, "What's the current yield?" That's the prospect back-pedaling into his old definitions and mistaking certainty for safety. Your answer is, of course, "The current yield will vary with the asset mix." In other words, if you like the fact that your assets can be moved around, out of harm's way and into the path of opportunity, you've got to accept that the current yield is going to move around as well. You don't buy an asset allocation fund for current yield anyway. You buy it for total return. Remember, it is exactly because today's current yields stepped on the prospect's airhose that you're having this conversation in the first place.

An obvious objection will be, "This fund will own stocks, and I don't want to own stocks." My response is, "That's not entirely true. You'd love to own stocks during major market uptrends and be mostly out of 'em during big downdrafts. Trouble is, you're never sure what the market is going to do. And, after 25 years, neither am I. That's why I'm not recommending a fully invested stock fund, or even a static, balanced fund. Gronsky Asset Allocation Fund offers you exposure to equities' higher returns, while taking you gradually to the sidelines when it looks like it's going to rain for awhile. Make sense?"

I think you see that the more relaxed you are about this—the more your attitude says, "Hey, I never know what these guys will do next either, but they've been mostly right, and that's all you can ask"—the easier it is to deflect questions and objections to which there are no hard answers anyway. Conversely, the more you try to blast every question/objection with a barrage of facts and figures, the more likely you are to drill yourself—and the sale—right into the ground.

Oh, and one last thing: Never, but *never*, use the phrase "asset allocation fund." Like all the industry jargon we love so much, it causes the risk-averse investor to immediately exhibit most or all of the major symptoms of a coma. Have a heart, guys (and do what the great salesperson always does): DON'T TELL 'EM WHAT IT *IS,* TELL 'EM *WHAT IT WILL DO FOR 'EM.*

One Over N:
The Formula For
Painless Prospecting

I've always felt that the central psychological problem of our profession isn't rejection, it's the way we experience rejection...which is a totally different (and infinitely more controllable) issue.

I also believe that prospecting and selling, far from being two points on the same continuum, are two entirely different sets of skills. "Selling is an art," I suggested in these two pieces: "prospecting...is a fairly exact science."

So, with a deep bow in the direction of Santa Ana, CA, home of "the Archdruid of behavior modification," Dr. Aaron Hemsley...here's the formula.

(In two installments, May & June, 1993)

One Over N: The Formula For Painless Prospecting

A couple of months ago, I got a call from a broker who was re-entering the business. He had read my book *Serious Money* as a way of getting re-acclimated. There was panic in his voice: "I have to get on the phone starting Monday and **your book doesn't tell me what to say!**"

One of my book's principal themes is that when it comes to prospecting, what you say is far less important than how many prospecting contacts you make. He couldn't accept that—such is the panic that prospecting arouses in us.

Some weeks later, while doing an all-day Saturday session I had been asked to give on prospecting, I was forced to think through my "belief system" about prospecting.

Nothing could have prepared me for what I encountered. The anger, the self-loathing, the guilt and the denial that immediately came to the surface stunned me. (In one session, a broker actually broke down and started to cry.) That's when I realized that I'd been in denial. Instead of writing about how to get in front of prospects, I'd written about what to say on the sales call.

So this will be the first of two columns devoted to the subject of prospecting. (You'll want to read/re-read Chapter 5, "Changing The Way You Keep Score" in my book *Serious Money: The Art of Marketing Mutual Funds* either before or along with reading these two columns.)

The Fundamental Principle

Let's start with the title of this article because it's the principle underlying all of my beliefs about prospecting. The title *says* "One Over N," but what it *means* is the fraction 1/N. It's the prospecting equivalent of $E=MC^2$, the basic law of the universe you and I live in.

It says that for every N prospecting contacts you make, you get a prospect. And that once you settle into your optimum style of prospecting, there isn't very much you can do or say to change N.

At this point, if you're anything like the folks I encountered at that Saturday session—if you haven't already gone ballistic—you're probably saying to yourself:

(a) So what the hell number is N?

(b) What's a prospecting contact? A dial? A cold call completion? An appointment? **What?**

(c) Is N different for me than the broker sitting next to me? How? Why?

(d) What's my optimum style of prospecting?

(e) What do you mean, you can't change N? **Tell me what to say!**

(f) All of the above.

Basic Principles Of Prospecting

See? I told you this was an emotional issue. So let's start all over again, from ground zero. Try to forget, at least for the moment, everything you think you know about prospecting. Because what you think you know probably isn't working, or you wouldn't be reading this column in the first place.

Here are some basic principles:

• **Prospecting is the ultimate numbers game.** It isn't an art (like selling); it's a science. So, it lends itself to an algebraic formula for success: 1/N. Your success will ultimately be measured not by who you called, or what you said, or what investments you recommended, or what "the market" did; but solely by *the number of prospective investors you spoke with.* Because every time you talk to N number of people, you get a prospect.

It has nothing whatsoever to do with your sales skills. How many times have you heard someone say (or heard *yourself* say): "You put me in front of a prospect, and I'll sell him; no problem." Or, "When I get an account, I can keep that account forever." We have great confidence in our selling and account management abilities; we simply can't pick up the phone and call new people. Which tells you that selling (which is a very high art form) and prospecting (an exact, remorseless, pitiless science) each requires a completely separate set of skills. (Remember, you read it here first.)

• **If you liked the game, you would play it all day long and you wouldn't want to go home for dinner.** But you hate the game, don't you? And who wants to play a game he hates?

The reason you hate the game is that *given the way you were taught to keep score,* you always lose. Your own success-driven internal guidance mechanisms, exacerbated by your sales training, tell you that when a prospect says yes—I'll take 1,000 shares, or you can call me again, or whatever—that's a good prospecting call. And when the prospect says no—where did you get my name, you felons are all alike, I hope your cat dies—that's a bad call.

Trouble is, if you accept the immutability of 1/N, then you are always going to get rejected (N-1) times for every prospect you get. If N is 15, for example, you have to be prepared to get rejected 14 times in order to get in front of one prospect. If you want two prospects, you have to get rejected 28 times. Three prospects, 42 rejections. And so on.

Under the old scorekeeping system, you have to experience 14 "bad calls" for every "good call." There's only one thing wrong with that. Fourteen rejections zero out your ego, and you go home, or to lunch with another salesperson, or to a saloon, or to look for Mrs. Gefarbnick's missing dividend check.

Nuts to that, you say. Wrong! Once you accept the inexorability of 1/N, then you want to get rejected as many multiples of (N-1) as you can. In other words, you'll think rejection is terrific, and you'll take as much of it as you can get. So the lesson to be learned from 1/N is, of course: A prospecting contact's outcome is completely immaterial. Every contact you make is a great success, simply because you made it. The only bad prospecting call is the one you do not make.

Reaching Your Goal

If a secretary says, "He doesn't take calls from salespeople," or an executive says, "I'm not interested" before you've given him anything not to be interested in, you have two options. You can let those responses hurt you and allow the cumulative buildup of that pain to stop you from prospecting; or you can view those rejections as putting you closer to your goal.

Someone who can't see the potential value to himself and his family of your years of experience in this business has no power to hurt you. Only you have the power to hurt you—if you elect to internalize this unthinking rejection, instead of saying (assuming you know that your N is 15), "Only 13 more rejections and I'll have my next prospect! God, I love this game!" You see, given the inexorable truth (and beauty) of 1/N, every rejection takes you one step closer to where you want to be.

If you learn some playfulness (this is, after all, a game) as you relax and make rejection your best friend, you may start saying some interesting, thought-provoking things. For instance, when the guy says, "I already have a broker," you'll respond, "Well, thank goodness! I'd never want to be anybody's first broker. What I want to be is *the last broker you ever do business with.*" Then you go on to tell him that, if he'll give you 20 minutes, you'll show him—at no cost to him—how you propose to do that.

Does the guy still say no? Hey, that's life. You'll feel great about yourself, and you only have 13 more bozos to go until you hit the statistically inevitable pay dirt.

Does your old scorekeeping system regard this contact as a failure? Gee, that's too bad. But you can live with it. Because you'll know that: You can experience an infinite number of "failures." But you can never *be* a failure, unless you stop prospecting. Which will only happen if you voluntarily elect to let the "failures" hurt you rather than teach you.

I don't believe there's anything on earth that you can do to change the incidence of rejection—to alter, in other words, the denominator in the fraction 1/N. There are no magic incantations you can utter, there's no great list you can buy, there's no 6-star Morningstar fund you can sell that is better than all other funds, and will vaporize all sales resistance.

You have total control, on the other hand, of how you *experience* rejection. Remember: You are incapable of making a "bad" prospecting contact. Because all contacts are good contacts, because...1/N.

Next month, I'll tell you how to find out what "N" is for you.

One Over N:
The Formula For
Painless Prospecting
(Part Deux)

In last month's column, I suggested that prospecting is the most daunting, anxiety-producing thing in our professional lives. No matter how confident we are in our ability to convince people once we get in front of 'em, it's the painful, rejection-riddled process of making the initial contact that we can't seem to master.

All of our sales training (such as it is) assumes—without ever explaining why—that prospecting, selling and account retention are all part of the same process. The thesis seems to be that these activities require the same set of attitudes and skills, that they're all points along the same continuum. I say that's ridiculous.

If you can sell anybody you can see—and lose accounts only to the undertaker—but can't pick up the phone to call new people, you know they're not the same skills. And, as is always the case when your training conflicts with your common sense life experience, your common sense is telling the truth.

Selling is an art—the highest art form many of us will ever practice. It's very personal, intuitive rather than logical, and intensely creative. Prospecting, on the other hand, is a fairly exact science, and one whose inexorable laws we have little or no power to change, no matter how creative we are. In other words, the 20-year veteran making 100 new approaches will probably experience almost exactly the same incidence of rejection as will a rookie, also calling (or calling on) 100 new people.

Are You Willing?

John Wayne's last movie, *The Shootist*, is about an old gunfighter dying of cancer. An adoring teenage boy, who's read of all Wayne's character's legendary gunfights, rhapsodizes about how fast on the draw he must have been in his prime. Wayne answers that being a great gunfighter isn't about how fast you are. "It's being *willing,*" he says.

That goes a long way toward explaining how I see prospecting. If the incidence of rejection that's implicit in the process doesn't change much, and it doesn't, the deciding factor must be how each of us experiences the rejection. If rejection corrodes you, you'll stop prospecting. If it fuels you—if you see it as a distasteful but inevitable means toward a highly desirable and perfectly pre-dictable end—you'll never stop playing the game. It's being *willing.*

So I postulate the immutable rule 1/N, which states that for every N number of prospecting approaches you make, you'll get a prospect. So, to get a prospect, all you ever have to do is be *willing* to get rejected N minus 1 times.

The Power Of N

Let's say that I know my N is 15. In other words, no matter how hard I try or how glibly I speak, I only get one prospect on average for every 15 contacts I make. *But I do get that one prospect.*

I'm all set. I'm going out there today and try my best to get reject-ed as many multiples of 14 (N-1, where N=15) as I can. Because whatever that multiple is, that's how many prospects I'm going to get. If I can manage to get rejected 42 times today (14 multiplied by three), I know I'm going to get three prospects. I may not get all three of 'em today—I might get two in a row, for no apparent rea-son, in my first few contacts tomorrow—but I know I'm gonna get 'em, and that's what keeps me going.

Finding Your Personal "N": The First Step

Simple, isn't it? Not easy, by any stretch of the imagination, but simple. So right about now, I'm guessing you can only find one thing wrong with it: you don't know what your own person-al N is.

Right. That's the problem. And the solution isn't to spend $300 on some all-day "motivational" seminar, after which you make 1300 calls Monday, 600 on Tuesday, 3 on Wednesday...and Thursday and

Friday you're out sick with a mysterious stomach ailment.

The solution is to find out what your N is. Because if you believe in 1/N (which is like saying, if you believe in Spring or baseball), and you know what your N is, you've got this business licked, once and for all.

And, since 1/N is a scientific fact, you need to solve for N dispassionately, scientifically. Get your ego out of it; get your emotions out of it. We're going to perform a clinical experiment here.

Edison tried at least 10,000 different wrong ways to produce an incandescent electric light before he hit what worked. After none of those 10,000 "failures" did he say, "I'm a bad person. I'm not cut out for this work. Somebody else is smart enough to figure it out, but not me." Et cetera. Edison *experienced* innumerable failures, but he could never *be* a failure because he never stopped experimenting. He knew he'd eventually figure it out, and in the meantime, he kept his ego and his emotions out of it!

The first thing you have to do in any scientific experiment is take notes, right? You have to record what's going on. And, oddly enough, that's the very first thing we stopped doing when our prospecting behavior began slowly tail-spinning toward the deck.

Remember how we all kept call sheets when we were first starting out? When did we stop doing that? And why, for heaven's sake?

I'll tell you why. Because, as the daily onslaught of rejection slowly took us down, the white spaces on those call sheets inched up from the bottom of the page until they all but overwhelmed it.

And, when we could no longer bear to look at all that empty space, we just stopped keeping call sheets altogether. We were veterans by now, after all; call sheets were for rookies. (As if, every day, we weren't unconsciously still carving those white spaces into our souls with a dull knife.)

So the road back starts with recording your activity—which is to say, it starts with being *willing* consciously to face your prospecting inactivity. (You can't overcome any problem unless/until you (a) say you have a problem and (b) stand ready to face the problem. Feverish, "motivation-driven" prospecting activity is merely another way of denying you have a problem.)

Finding Your Personal "N": The Second Step

The question now becomes: What are we going to record? Our shame-based, self-recriminatory belief system says we've only performed a real prospecting behavior when we've actually talked to the prospect himself. I don't buy that.

Say I pick up the phone, call a specific lead, and get his assistant. The assistant (a) will not put a salesman through to Mr. Big and (b) passes along Mr. Big's devout hope that I, and every one of my kind, may starve to death in the dark.

That, to me, even if it doesn't include the starving-to-death part, is a prospecting behavior. It's a hash mark on my call sheet. It's one of my 14 rejections. I *love* this call!

You see, I'm conducting a career-long experiment. I'm trying to find those 1000 or so people, out of 250 million Americans, who are going to be my clients and friends for the rest of my life. My call to Mr. Big was an enormous success, in the best Edisonian sense. Because the guy informed me, categorically if not in person, that he's ineligible to be one of the 1000. Pity. **Next!**

Note that part of the reason this works is that I'm taking a long-term perspective—career-long, to be precise. If you're trying to change your prospecting activity so you can get more accounts so you can do more business so you can pay for a vacation you're planning to take this August...it ain't gonna work.

You got into the habit of prospecting inactivity very slowly, and you're going to change that habit slowly. There is no wealth without risk, there is no 30-pounds-in-30-days-without-dieting weight-loss plan, and there is no major, lasting, but overnight alteration in prospecting behavior. So relax. It's a process; it doesn't come in cans, like Popeye's spinach. I say again: relax. In a very real way, this recovery process starts when you climb down off your own back.

OK, so we've decided that each approach you make verbally—in person or over the phone—is a prospecting behavior. (Secretary says: "He's in Guam. Call back Tuesday." By my scorekeeping method, I get a hash mark, even if the secretary then says, "He's in Borneo. Call back next St. Swithin's Day.")

See, I can't control where the guy is. I can only control my prospecting behavior. I performed the behavior that inevitably leads to success: I called on the phone, or knocked on the door, or whatever, I did what I'm supposed to do, and I get rewarded with a hash mark.

If I keep score this way, doesn't that inevitably inflate my N? In other words, if I count "He's in Guam" or even "He's on the other wire" as hash marks, don't I have to make that many more approaches/hash marks to get one prospect? Sure, but that feels OK to me. I love to—and apparently need to—see that growing army of hash marks marching across my call sheet all day, every day. That's what fuels me.

You might still say, "It's only a hash mark if I talk to the guy." Well, that's very noble of you, in a puritanical, self-flagellating sort of way. But I guarantee, when you go through a whole morning of constantly dialing the phone, listening to he's-in-Sarawak-he's-on-the-other-wire-he-doesn't-take-calls-from-pond-scum-like-you, and you haven't got a hash mark to your name by lunch time, you're gonna put the phone through a wall and go off this program. *Guaranteed.*

(Still, if you've got another scorekeeping system that works better for you, that you can stick to, by all means be my guest. Your system is better than mine, because it works for you. There are no rules; there's only *what works for you.* If you wanted a life of externally imposed rules, you picked the wrong business—you should have joined the Army.)

Finding Your Personal "N": The Third Step

Next: how many hash marks do you need each day to start with? Same answer: your guess is every bit as good as mine, and probably much better because you know you and I don't, and in the end it has to be your system.

Dr. Aaron Hemsley, who is to me the Archdruid of behavior modification, suggests that we start by merely making a prospecting approach whenever we feel like it, and record those hash marks. Don't do it when you feel you "should" ("should" by whose rules anyway?). You'll feel and sound strained, which reinforces the bad vibes on both ends of the phone. Do a prospecting behavior only when you feel really good about doing a prospecting behavior. You'll sound good because you feel good, rather than sounding like somebody who's running the gauntlet, and this call is the 44th tomahawk blow of the day.

Do this for a week, says Hemsley, and then average the number of hash marks you got over the whole week. (Don't bother counting the prospects yet. (A) You may not have gotten any. (B) That's the old results-oriented scorekeeping system that corroded your soul to begin with. The behaviors, the hash marks themselves, are the winning experiences.)

Take that average number of hash marks and try to do that exact number—no more, unless you really feel like it, *but no less*—each day for two weeks. If you can sustain that number each and every day for ten working days, you've found what Hemsley calls your "baseline"—that number of positive prospecting behaviors you can consistently perform without running afoul of your anxiety.

If you can't sustain that number, drop down one and see if you can sustain *that* for ten days. Keep doing this until you get down to that bedrock, sustainable baseline number.

Wherever your baseline is, when you've done it for ten working days (*each and every day*, not on average), add one behavior a day and see if you can sustain *that* level for ten days. You can? OK, add one more behavior, and repeat this experiment for ten more days.

Train, don't strain. We're increasing our prospecting behavior so gradually here that our rejection-shocked, anxiety-ridden unconscious may not notice!

How many prospects have we got? What's our N? Who the hell knows and, much more important, who cares? You're never going to know what N is until you have a large enough sample of calls to judge from. And you're never going to have that large, statistically meaningful sample of calls until you *slowly but surely* build your prospecting activity back up to the point where the numbers reliably tell you something. It's a two-phase process.

Don't even start recording the number of prospects until after the first 90 days of baseline experimentation. For those first 90 days, the baseline work must be an end in itself. Building that consistent behavior pattern—no matter from what low level it starts—is the key to everything.

(Consistency is like milk: You never outgrow your need for it. At least I don't. I do all major projects in 90-day clips, and they all are based on the same level of performance every single day. I wrote my book *Serious Money* five manuscript pages a day— more when I felt like it, but never less. That's why it only took four months to write. It took 24 years to upload, in other words. But, at a rate of five yellow legal pages a day, it only took four months to download.)

For the second 90 days, as you continue to try to build up your baseline, you can start recording the number of prospects you get. In the next two clips of 90 days—in other words, nine months after Day One—you will know precisely what N is.

Nine months is too long, you say? Apparently nature doesn't think so when she creates a new human being. (And if you don't think this process creates an entirely new and different you, then I just don't know what to tell you.) If you'll give it those nine months—calmly, slowly, consistently, non-judgmentally, with your ego and emotions well out of it—you will quite literally be set for life. Prospecting will become a lifelong, joyful game which—since you already know you're going to win 1/N times—you'll never stop playing.

A *Postscript:* My six-o'clock-news-sound-bite summary of Aaron Hemsley's work really doesn't begin to do him justice. I believe that every one of us needs to get familiar with Aaron's work and incorporate it into our professional lives. I'd start with Aaron's basic tape series, "The Psychology of Maximum Sales Production," which you can order by calling 714-832-6109.

Proof Positive:
You Make A Difference

I've always felt that the no-load fund industry—
aided and abetted by journalism—had framed the
debate in the wrong terms. They said that the
central issue in a lifetime of investing was which
funds you bought. And, everything else being
equal, a no-load fund should "outperform" a load
fund—if only by the difference of the load.

Nobody who's ever worked with the
individual investor for any length of time
believes this. Instead, we know that which
mutual funds an investor buys has virtually no
effect on his long-term investment return. What
counts is **what the investor does with his funds
after he buys 'em**. And that, in turn, is almost
always a function of the quality of the advice the
investor gets—or, in the case of no-load funds,
doesn't get. (Which is why, a while ago, I
stopped calling them "load" and "no-load"
funds. I think it's much more accurate to call
them "help" and "no-help" funds.)

That's why I was so glad to see the ICI study
discussed in this column, which proved the
existence of very large differences in the holding
periods of "help" vs. "no-help" funds...to the
clear advantage of "help" funds. The study also
showed that "no-help" fund buyers were much
more likely to bail out because of current
events/falling markets/malaise du jour concerns.
"In other words," I wrote,

"AS HE'S DONE FROM TIME IMMEMORIAL, THE
LONELY, SCARED, UNADVISED INVESTOR GOT
CAUGHT UP IN THE JOURNALISM-INDUCED
MALAISE DU JOUR. AND BLEW COMPLETELY
OUT OF HIS **LONG-TERM** INVESTMENTS
BECAUSE OF SOME **SHORT-TERM** BOGEYMAN."

The other ICI study I commented on here was
one which tended to bear out everything I'd been
saying about toxic definitions of risk and safety.
This, again, was something I believe people need
a professional to explain to them, because they
won't figure it out on their own until it's too late.

All in all, I felt that these two studies struck a
blow for the good ...

Proof Positive: You Make A Difference

Whether you're one of those people who refuses to believe studies, or one of those folks who's reassured by them, you'll find two studies the Investment Company Institute recently released very interesting and potentially useful in your practice. Both studies address major themes you've read about in this column—as well as in my book, *Serious Money*—over the last year or so.

The first of the two studies, *Understanding Shareholder Redemption Decisions,* provides the statistical backup for something you and I have always known. That is, investors who buy funds using a compensated professional advisor probably do better—or at least make certain critical mistakes less often—than people who buy funds on their own.

The second, even more voluminous study, *Piecing Together Shareholder Perceptions of Investment Risk*, proves empirically (at heaven only knows what cost) something that I have written about in this column periodically over the last several years. Namely, that "risk is one of the more misunderstood principles of investing."

The "risk study" demonstrates, in its own words, that "most investors look at financial risk as the potential to lose principal," period. A secondary finding, which echoes another of this column's frequent themes, is that "a shareholder's family history can influence his or her investment behavior and tolerance for financial risk." Though both findings may strike you as the understatements of the millennium, the point is: **now you have proof.**

De-Bunking The No-Load Myth

The ICI study that examines shareholder redemption decisions hits die-hard proponents of "do-it-yourself investing" squarely between the eyes. Those folks—principally journalists—have systematically tried to convince individual investors over the last decade or so that only the addle-brained need to hire someone to help them make decisions about which mutual funds to buy.

As you and I both know, there are a lot of people out there who need help making investment decisions, and one of the most popular ways—but by no means the only way—to compensate you (a trained professional) for that help is by paying a commission.

In the "old days" (in this case, that's just a few years ago), this debate was as simple as whether you bought a "load" or a "no-load" mutual fund. Since the introduction of so-called B, C, and D shares, the distinction between load and no-load funds has blurred. Add to that the fact that some financial advisors choose to receive a fee rather than a commission for their advice, and the no-load versus load debate further blurs.

Semantics aside, the unspoken, unexamined underlying journalistic hypothesis behind the "no-load argument" is, of course, that investors will do equally well (or equally badly) in either type of fund, so why pay a sales charge when you don't have to?

The critical fallacy here is the notion that *investment* returns and *investor* returns are the same—that the investor, *unaided*, will behave rationally, stay focused on the long term, and let the basic uptrend carry him to his destination.

The ICI's redemption study clearly suggests that this hypothesis must not (as you and I have always known it cannot) be true. Because it documents (I believe for the first time) radical differences in the behavior of fund redeemers who paid to buy their fund shares and those who were "direct marketed." (By the way, direct marketed has to be by far the best euphemism for "no-load" I've heard thus far.)

"Full Redeemers"

The ICI surveyed people who redeemed all or part of their mutual fund accounts in the ten months ending in March of 1992. For purposes of this discussion, I'd like to focus on the people the study refers to as "full redeemers"—those who heeded the dictum of the Amityville Horror and GOT OUT...lock, stock and fund account.

"Direct-market" full redeemers were **twice as likely** as salesforce redeemers to sell all their fund shares within two years of purchase! They didn't do the one essential thing you have to do—particularly in equities—in order to be successful; give them enough time to work.

Why not? There are no doubt a variety of reasons. But one of them has to be that there was no investment professional like you telling those direct-market, full redeemers how important it is to **just hang in there,** and give the long-term uptrend time to do its glorious (and totally inevitable) work.

You see, anybody can *buy* an equity mutual fund. The point is that, without professional help, many investors won't stay in the fund.

Can You Fly This Plane?

In other words, buying an equity mutual fund turns out to be a lot like buying an airplane. In a no-load fund, the investor buys the plane. Period. He doesn't pay for, and does not get, the services of a pilot. The question therefore becomes: **Are you absolutely sure you know how to fly this plane?**

When the investor buys a fund with a sales charge (or a fee, or whatever), he gets a plane **and** a pilot. So sit back, relax, and have another screw-top Chardonnay: the pilot will get you where you're going (that is, if you let him).

That's not to suggest that paying someone a commission or a fee guarantees investment success. Clearly, it doesn't. Even if the investor pays for a pilot, he can still dash up to the cockpit in a storm, knock the pilot unconscious, grab the controls himself, and drill the plane into the side of a mountain! (Also, in all fairness, paying for advice doesn't insulate the investor from the risk that the person giving that advice will turn out to be a jerk.)

The ICI study also found that, of all the full redeemers who bailed out of the plane primarily because they were "concerned about investment conditions or market climate," 32% were direct-market buyers versus only 19% salesforce buyers. In other words, as he's done from time immemorial, the lonely, scared, unadvised investor got caught up in the journalism-induced *malaise du jour.* And blew completely out of his long-term investments because of some short-term bogeyman.

(These days, of course, crisis lovers have to subsist on pretty thin soup—stuff like Hillary's healthcare plan, or Bubba's budget. Can it be only 20 Octobers ago when, **in one week,** the price of oil tripled and the vice president of the United States pleaded *nolo contendere* to a felony and resigned? All while we were holding off a monolithic thermonuclear enemy. Call me an old fogey, but we had real *malaises* back in them *jours.*)

Why did only 19% of salesforce buyers make the same mistake? Again, there are probably several reasons. But a big one has to be that the pilot they retained got on the intercom and, in his best Chuck Yeager drawl, told 'em they'd just hit a big ol' patch of clear air turbulence, and not to fret none, on account of how we're gonna come out on the other side of it (jes like we always do) in the battin' of an eye.

So, now you have (as if you need it) statistical evidence that your advice makes a real difference. Mutual funds are *not* a commodity, to be purchased at the lowest price. **You gotta have a pilot.**

Blame It On Your Parents

The ICI's other study, which focuses on shareholders perceptions of risk, proves beyond a shadow of a doubt what you read here first: Folks get their notions of risk from their family background.

Because so many of my columns over the last year or so have dealt with the subject of risk—and redefining it (*Stop Selling, Start Redefining*, August '92; *Conquering Prospects' Fear With Four Questions (And Two Postage Stamps)*, February '93; *Battling Toxic Definitions Syndrome*, April '93)—I'm loath to beat it into the ground like a tomato stake. That said, let's spend a few minutes on these issues. Because, once again, you make the difference.

We're all, directly or through genetic encoding, children of the Depression. Either we're old enough to be carrying that wound from our direct experience, or we're not—in which case we got the wound from our parents. (That's why it's so tough for you to reason with investors concerning risk. In a very real sense, you're contradicting everything your prospect's mother and father told him.)

Generalizing from a massive, horrific, but ultimately momentary episode in which everybody lost his principal, our folks taught us that risk was principal. And, as the ICI study demonstrates, we all still believe it.

Thirty years ago, when our fathers (or grandfathers) retired at 65 and died at 72, this probably wasn't as pernicious a fallacy as it is now. But today, when people are retiring at 60 and living another quarter century, the obsession with principal (which I call "yesterday's risk") is literally killing people financially.

And if the saver/investor can't even conceive that there *is* another risk, he certainly can't imagine that another risk—purchasing power—actually dwarfs the risk that he'll lose his money. Nor, without your help, is he likely to figure this out on his own...at least, not before it's too late.

You have to show people (and richly deserve your compensation for doing so) that *risk has changed because life has changed.* Our retirement ages, our life expectancies, are radically different from those of our parents. We won't make it if we save and invest as they did. The old truths are not only *not* the best truths...they aren't even true anymore!

The trouble is that most investors, in terms of their life's financial journey, are already up there at 36,000 feet...and they've never had a flying lesson. (Their folks could only teach 'em how to drive a car, remember?)

You're the pilot. You're worth whatever it costs to bring these folks safely home. But if you don't see that—or won't stand up for it—I don't know how you can expect your clients to accept it.

Coming Face-To-Face With The Universal Objection

*By the summer of '93, with stock and bond markets soaring, the universal objection—"the market's too high"—was once again abroad in the land. In this column, I made the point that people don't really know whether the market's too high or not, but it gives them a convenient way **to avoid having to make a decision**. It's one of those tar-baby arguments that, the harder you hit it, the more you get stuck. And it isn't even the real objection; **it's a proxy for something else.***

*So I went back to The Three Patriot Missiles of Q&A (from **Serious Money**) to gently show people that, for the great preponderance who aren't finished accumulating their investments yet, a Big Sale (what amateurs call a "bear market") would be just what the doctor ordered.*

Coming Face-To-Face With The Universal Objection

The nearly universal objection du jour to equity investing is, "The market's too high." It's one of those arguments prospects love to raise because, of course, there's no objective answer to it.

You won't know whether the market is too high or not until much later—and in the meantime, your prospect will have gotten out of having to make a decision. (Later, of course, when the market is much higher—as it always is—your prospect will get to say, "Can't buy now. Too late." But I digress.)

It's important that you realize the prospect isn't necessarily opposed to investing in equities. He's opposed to **having to make a decision.** But no one can ever say that to a salesman or planner, so they dream up a proxy objection. And today it's "The market's too high."

The Wrong Variable

The absolute worst thing you can do is debate this objection on its own merits, because it's a quagmire (and the prospect knows it; that's why he said it). Moreover, like the load objection, it's a classic example of a debate that's being framed around the wrong variable.

The load objection, as a I pointed out in last month's column, assumes that the critical variable in equity fund performance is what your client paid (or didn't pay) to buy the fund. But that's not the issue at all. Anybody can buy an equity fund; very few people can keep one through a frightening, bitter market decline, of the kind you get about every five years. You add value by waking your client out of that nightmare, by reminding him that all equity market declines are temporary—no matter how permanent they look when you're in the middle of one. If you isolate purely on the front-end costs, you'll miss this point entirely.

Same with "the market's too high." The "height" of the market isn't the critical issue, but rather **what does the investor need to accomplish and what is his time horizon for accomplishing it?**

For instance, say you're prospecting a 50-year-old couple looking to retire at 62. They're sitting with 70% to 80% of their money in short-to-intermediate term debt and can put away another $3,000 a month for the next 144 months. Clearly, equities are their only hope for a decent life, so who cares where the market is? And yet we find that folks like these are obsessed with whether the market's too high. Why? Because they've got the debate framed around the wrong issues.

First of all, they're worried about "losing their money" in stocks. But how, exactly, does one do that? These folks don't know; they just believe it can happen. (This issue only *appears* to be one of ignorance; the central issue is fear. Remember: the antidote to fear isn't information, it's **trust.**)

Fear makes you subscribe to the myth of the possibility of permanent decline, even though the story of your life is a permanent advance. Sixty-one years ago this summer the DJIA was 40; today it's around 3600. Again, how do you lose money in a market like that? Well, it isn't easy, but it can be done.

All you have to do is mistake a temporary decline (which we get all the time: 10% about every two years, 25% about every five) for a permanent decline (which we **never** get). And bail out, at or near the bottom.

The other mistaken belief around which our 50-year-olds are framing the debate is that stock price declines are always bad. I'd argue that a nice 35%-or-so hit over the next few years would be about the best thing that could happen to these folks.

That's because they're going to be dollar-cost-averaging over the next 144 months. And dollar-cost-averaging (the market-timing system God would use if She didn't already know the future) works even better *the more the market gets hit*. These people aren't (or shouldn't be) trying to pile up *dollars* right now; they should be piling up *shares*. The more the market temporarily declines, the more *shares* their $3,000 a month will buy.

So, in a very real sense, when these folks look at you in fear and say, "The market's too high," your answer has to be, "I certainly hope so, for your sakes."

Turning The Objection On Its Ear

If you've read my book *Serious Money*, the last 71 pages of which are devoted to questions/objections handling, you'll have recognized the above response as a non-answer answer—one of my "Three Patriot Missiles of Q & A."

You see, we know that objections like "The market's too high" are not framed in useful terms, and may not even be the real objection (but rather a proxy therefor). So the one 100%-reliably-wrong thing we can do is answer the objection as stated.

Instead, you lob in one of the Three Patriot Missiles, which are:

(1) The non-answer answer

(2) Answering with a question

(3) Why?

In other words, you find a nice, gentle, non-argumentative (but lethal) way of turning the issue back on the prospect. You signal him in the strongest possible way that the issue doesn't concern you, and that, properly examined, it soon won't concern him either.

You never argue. (A) You don't know what the market's going to do. (B) All arguments in a sales context (like those concerning religion and politics) are unwinnable. (C) What if the stated issue isn't the real issue?

Variations On A Theme

Let's go through each of the Patriot Missile variations to see how each one works mechanically, but also to bolster your own belief system. (Because, in the end, your prospects aren't moved by what you know: They're moved by what you believe.)

1. Answering with the non-answer answer.

Prospect: "Market's too high."

Superstar: "I certainly hope so, for your sakes." (Silence.)

Prospect: "HUH?"

Superstar: "Well, we've agreed that staying in low-yielding debt isn't an option for you folks, and that only the rising dividend stream from owning great companies can protect your purchasing power in retirement.

So, over the next 144 months, you're going to be stocking up on shares of great companies, through Gronsky Growth & Income Fund.

Now, you're saying those shares are going to go on sale somewhere down the road, because they're "too high" just at the moment. And I hope you're right, and that your $3,000 a month will catch some big sales.

But we can't be sure. In fact, I can make a pretty good case that, as the world explodes into global capitalism, we ain't seen nothin' yet. Who's right? We'll know in five or ten years.

But by then it'll be too late for you. And this isn't really a conversation about the market. It's a conversation about you. The risk isn't that the market is about to put on one of its every-five-years, 25%-off sales. (That's an *opportunity*.) The risk is that, for every one of the remaining 144 months that you stay in 4% debt, your goals fade further into the mist.

The journey of 144 months begins with a single month...see what I mean?"

2. Now let's look at answering with a question.

Prospect: "Market's too high."

Superstar: "Too high for what...or whom?" (Silence.)

Prospect: "HUH?"

Superstar: "I guess I'm asking: what does the level of the market *today* have to do with your retirement, 144 months from today?"

Prospect: "Well, uh...I don't know...doesn't it being at all-time highs scare you, with the deficit and taxes and everything?"

Superstar: "I'm more scared—on your behalf—of watching you lose any of these 144 precious months to a 4% debt market.

The thing is: You have to pick what you're going to be scared of. Your retirement is *certain*. A sale on the great companies—because right now they're "too high"—is a *possibility*.

First of all, I think you have to invest against certainty. Then you can hedge against possibilities. And, of course, by systematically investing over the next 144 months, **you hedge perfectly against all possibilities.**

If the prices of great companies go up—which they do 70% to 80% of the time—you own, every month, a bigger and bigger chunk of an appreciating asset.

If the prices of great companies go on sale—and there's a 25%-off sale on an average of every five years—you'll pick up a lot of extra shares. With a little luck, you'll see that happen two or three times before you retire.

You're a winner either way—as long as you don't gum up a *long-term* program of acquiring great companies because of *short-term* market concerns.

See what I mean?"

3. Lastly, we'll look at all-purpose, all-weather, always-reliable "Why?"

Prospect: "Market's too high."

Superstar: "Why?" (Silence.)

Prospect: "HUH? Uh, price/earnings, price/book, etc., etc."

Superstar: "What's the worst that can happen?"

Prospect: "The market can crash!"

Superstar: "No; for you that's the *best* that can happen. I asked: What's the *worst* that can happen?"

Prospect: "HUH?"

Superstar: "Somebody who's accumulating shares of great companies over a decade or more—like you—wants all the crashes he can get. They're like fire sales.

I admit, if you had to decide what to do with all your money today, short-term market movements would be a somewhat valid concern. That's why patient accumulators like you and me are in a much better position than some poor guy who's really rich *now*.

So, for purposes of your 144-month, $3,000-a-month program, I hope you're right that the market's going to crack.

My fear is that the market's right—it usually is—and that it's focusing on exploding global capitalism rather than on today's P/E ratio. After all, the P isn't wrong if the E is about to go on a tear...which it may very well be.

I appreciate your concern. Anything that's been going up all our lives—as the great companies have been—always looks high *if you're looking back*. But if you're looking *ahead*, as the great investor always does...well, you see what I mean, don't you?"

* * * * *

Boys and girls, let's help investors wake up and smell the pizza. Most of our clients are (or ought to be) accumulators. And so are most of us. So to them, it's good if the market's not too high...but even better if it is.

Let me close with a personal observation. I was born in 1943, so I'm a child of the Bomb, and of the Cold War. The other day, on a flight from Toronto to Calgary, I heard the pilot on the P.A. "extend a special welcome to the contingent of Russian businessmen flying with us this morning."

And I thought, *"Russian businessmen."* Five years ago, that phrase was an oxymoron. Ten years ago, it was a capital offense.

Folks, I don't know whether the market's "too high" at the moment or not. But if stuff like "Russian businessmen" doesn't make you a long-term bull, either you're much, **much** smarter than I am...or you're brain dead.

Getting Ready
For The Fall

I probably had more speaking engagements in the spring and summer of 1993 than I'd ever had in a comparable period. And, as I traveled around the country, I began to get very, very bad vibes.

*My long-term bullishness was (and is) as rampant as ever. But I became convinced that the markets—and far too many investment reps— were simply too sanguine. The business was being fueled by short-term interest rates at 30-year lows; indeed, as the column pointed out, the **real** short-term interest rate was zero. (A) I didn't see how rates could go lower than zero, and (B) it was clear to me that, given the way the economy was booming, the Fed was going to have to rein it in sooner than later.*

*So, for the first time—and with a lot of trepidation that shows clearly in the article—I did sort of a bearish piece. "All my years," I wrote, "tell me we're cruisin' for a bruisin' ." And, once again inadvertently, I hit the absolute tippy-top of the bond market. (Stocks, always capable of **much** more wretched excess than bonds, didn't top out for another four months.)*

The article listed ten things reps could do to put their business into a more defensive posture. "Sit down with your business plan, and/or your book," I said, "and assume you're about to be attacked."

Perhaps because I had the courage to trust my instincts and go against the grain of my own relentless long-term bullish posture, I'm more proud of this piece than of any other in this book.

Getting Ready For The Fall

Ah, the blissful pleasures of a bull-market summer.

There's nothing quite like having your business boom during the sunshine months. You can really get out and make the most of the human tendency to goof off when business is easy to come by.

Prospecting? Well, everybody was away in the summer; we promised ourselves we'd start cranking again after Labor Day. But now, with business still rolling in and the weather still beautiful (and the crowds gone), it feels really good to check out at noon on Fridays, and maybe take Mondays off.

One by one, the good habits you built up when business was tough get put on hold. When does this happen? Right before The Fall...in both senses of the term.

And how about the markets (whose good graces we have come to rely on perhaps more than on our own energy and discipline)? Well, the stock market takes roughly a 10% hit on an average of once every two years. And we had our last one in the third quarter of 1990...just about three years ago. Moreover, stocks take a 25% dive about every 5 1/2 years (at least since the end of WWII). And we had our last one of those from August through October of 1987. And, let's see, that was...six years ago. Hmmm.

Meanwhile, over in the debt markets, we've entered our thirteenth year of the greatest secular bull market in history. Nominal short-term interest rates have rallied from 15% to under 3%. And *real* short-term rates, as Alan Greenspan recently pointed out to Congress, have actually rallied to zero. (Three percent nominal rates minus 3% inflation equals zip.) On the long end, the 30-year Treasury bond went to 6.1% last month.

Finally, mutual fund sales have soared to staggering levels. Mr.

and Mrs. America may not really *like* stocks (woe betide us when they do). But when the clock struck midnight and the golden coach of their "investments" (10% Treasuries! Yes!) turned back into the pumpkin of **savings** (You'll renew my CD at two point **what**?!), folks didn't have much choice.

So let's add up what we've got here. Business booming, and real easy to come by. Work ethic slackening significantly. Everything you buy is up a month later. And up more the month after that. The public pouring money into stock and bond investments. And one thing I forgot to mention: sales training programs running flat out, as thousands of new college graduates who can't find jobs elsewhere head for Wall Street, banks, and life insurance companies.

Cruisin' For A Bruisin'

Call me an old fogey—you're going to anyway, so go ahead and get it out of your system. But the foregoing paragraph is a litany of just about everything I've learned to hate and fear. All my years tell me we're cruisin' for a bruisin'. And that it's getting overdue.

Now, before you go ballistic on me, please remember:

1. No one, and I mean no one, is more of a long-term bull than I am. And the long term is all that really matters, provided you can keep clients focused on it.

We're witnessing the outbreak of a global capitalist revolution. Remember my mantra, "Russian businessmen," from last month's column ("Coming Face-To-Face With The Universal Objection"). Plus, the demographics of the greying baby boomers spell the great gettin'-up morning of the investment business. If you ain't a long-term bull today, I sincerely believe that's a sign from God that She sent you into the world to sell bond funds. It's not the long term I'm worried about; it's the next bend in the river.

2. I'm not trying to call short-term turns in the markets. Nobody can reliably do that. And if anybody could, it wouldn't be me. (Although, I have to say, the one time I tried to do it in this column was October 1990—in the article called "Selling Skills For Recessionary Times"—and I hit one out of the park in straightaway center.)

I don't think the market is, in any meaningful sense, "too high."

(The trailing 12-month P/E of the S&P 500 has crashed in the last year, from 28 to a little north of 22, for instance.) And even if it is, a dollar-cost-averaging accumulator—like me—always welcomes a sale on the great companies.

Also, I'm somewhat comforted by the amount of public and professional fear that's around. Marty Zweig recently called this "the market everybody loves to hate." I want very much to believe that, and yet those mutual fund sales keep booming!

3. I can't even put my finger on what bothers me. It's just this relentless accumulation of little bad signs, which may or may not agglomerate to one big bad sign. I feel like the old Indian scout in a 1940s John Ford western. You know, where the West-Point-by-the-book cavalry captain says, "Nice and quiet out here on the plains tonight." And the scout says, "Yeah. *Too* quiet."

Planning For The Fall

I'm not sounding battle stations. I'm just suggesting that we shorten our sails and double the guard. And that we get started sooner than later. In case you hadn't noticed, October isn't just hurricane season in the Caribbean. Three of the last six Octobers ('87, '89 and '90) got pretty blowy around the corner of Broad and Wall, too.

My specific recommendations:

1. Play War Games—Sit down with your business plan, and/or your book, and assume you're about to be attacked. Suppose there's a 50% chance of a 10% market hit in the next 12 months. (Or a 25% chance of a 25% market hit. Or a 50-basis-point back-up in long rates. Or whatever.) Now ask: Which clients would be hardest hit by that? Which funds? Which stock or bond positions? Talk to the overexposed clients; cut back on the positions that are vulnerable.

2. Share Your Concerns With Clients—Don't scare 'em, but don't play Superman, either. Real people value prudence in their investment advisor, and it draws them closer to you. If you have accounts with whom you feel the need to be a raging bull or they'll go elsewhere…let 'em go now. They're going to be lost anyway. You'll need your strength and energy to manage your real long-term relationships if a storm hits. Take a moment now to put a couple of crazies in a lifeboat and cut 'em loose.

Ask your clients and prospects what, if anything, *they're* concerned about. I never heard a client complain that his investment advisor was asking too many good questions.

3. Shorten Maturities—People always say they want safety and income. But, in my experience, what they really want is a lot of income and the illusion of safety. So there are too many people pouring way too much money into long government bond funds today.

Start a phone campaign based on the theme of "What you *may* really need is *lower* yields." If nothing else, you'll sure get people's attention.

4. Raise A Little Cash—Take tax losses now. Don't reinvest all the proceeds from a called bond.

Or, vector your new money coming in toward funds whose managers historically are willing to build up relatively large cash positions. Lots of stock funds are always 90% to 95% invested, because the managers feel (quite legitimately) that their job is to pick stocks, not time the market. And that, particularly if you're dollar-cost-averaging, is what you want 'em to do.

But do your clients know that's the plan? And are they emotionally in shape for it? If so, fine. If not, maybe you want to look for more defensive managers.

5. Concentrate On Value-Oriented, Dividend-Paying Stocks and Funds. Add A Convertible Bond Fund To Your Equity Fund Portfolio—They'll go down somewhat less in a general market decline. Plus, the dividends (whether spent or reinvested) have a calming effect on nervous investors, and make them more inclined to ride out a decline...which is all you ever have to do to be a successful investor.

6. Stop—Just Completely Stop—Selling Track Record—Track-record selling fosters greed, when what we need to do, if I'm right, is foster a little healthy fear. The more heavily an investor bases his "buy" decision on track record, the more likely he is to panic and sell out at exactly the wrong time.

7. Look For Something To Short, Or Buy A Put—In a way, this is just a reality check. Something is always vulnerable, no matter how good the market is. If you can't get clients to be on the short side/put side of *something*, with 2 1/2% to 5% of their accounts, we're in even worse trouble than I thought.

8. Start Emphasizing Funds/Annuities With Back-End Loads and/or Surrender Charges—These days, a lot of investors who are getting their equity exposure from mutual funds really should be getting it (tax deferred) from annuities, and even from variable life insurance.

Mutual funds are real easy to sell out of; these products aren't. If markets get hit, the client's visceral unwillingness to pay the surrender charge may accomplish what all our pleading can't—keeping him hanging in there.

9. Get Referrals—The approach is, "You see that I'm being cautious and prudent on your behalf; don't you have a really close friend or associate who *deserves* the same kind of care?"

10. Get Back To Work—What time would you get into the office if 25% of your money line had just melted away in the night? And what time did you actually get in this morning? The greater the time between those two answers, the more potential trouble you're in.

To do best, assume the worst. "Sweet are the uses of adversity," as Shakespeare said...even if the adversity never happens.

The No-Load Cardiologist

In August, 1993, I got sicker than I've been in years, with a throat infection so painful I felt like I was swallowing razor blades. It was initially misdiagnosed, so I spent a couple of days on the wrong antibiotic—getting worse instead of better.

At times like this, when I feel hopeless and without sufficient resources to cope, I always say the serenity prayer over and over again ("God, grant me the serenity to accept the things I cannot change, the courage to change the things I can, and the wisdom to know the difference"). I find that I can stay all riled up emotionally, or I can keep saying the serenity prayer...but not both. This particular day, the serenity prayer won. And as I was lying there calmly, a voice in my head said, "The no-load cardiologist." I said, "What?" And the voice said, "That's right: Dr. Murray Murray, the no-load cardiologist."

I must have recently seen the movie "The Sunshine Boys," about two old vaudevillians getting together to do their classic "doctor sketch" one last time. Because a doctor sketch of a no-load cardiologist basically wrote itself over the next couple of hours. I think it's the single funniest thing (with a deadly serious, if satiric, message) I ever wrote.

Later, the State Mutual Life/Allmerica Financial companies had a professionally produced video made of this sketch, with a very gifted comic actor as the patient...and yours truly as Dr. Murray Murray. If you do business with them, ask 'em to show you the video sometime. I know I'm not objective, but I think it's a scream.

The serious point, of course, is how deeply counterintuitive the no-load myth is. The idea that virtually anyone can put in place **and keep in place** a successful lifetime investment program isn't reasonable, much less probable. Americans are not instinctively good investors— indeed, as I've said elsewhere, they're not investors at all. They're savers. And it's extremely improbable that the average American saver can, without help, become a good investor.

We offer that help, and we earn our compensation for rendering that help. That's the ultimate message of "The No-Load Cardiologist."

The No-Load Cardiologist

The scene opens in a doctor's office, replete with diploma, the obligatory skeleton hanging in the corner, a blood pressure cuff mounted on the wall, an exam table covered with white paper and the other trappings that signify the practice of medicine.

The lights come up as the office door opens. An extremely worried-looking patient, glancing nervously about, is shown into the office by an intelligent, well-read, intellectually independent nurse.

Nurse: If you'll just have a seat on the examining table, the doctor will be with you in just a moment. (Exits)

Doctor: (Enters stage left, staggers across stage, applies stethoscope to skeleton.) Ah, good morning! Went a little too far on that liquid diet, did we?

Patient: Doctor, I'm over here.

Doctor: And not looking much better, either! Well, how are you feeling?

Patient: Actually, doctor, I'm feeling very poorly.

Doctor: Ah! What seems to be the trouble?

Patient: Well, I have this terrific tightness in my chest, mostly on the left side. I'm very short of breath. And I have a lot of pain in my left arm. Do you think it's my heart?

Doctor: Sure sounds like it, sonny. So you've come to the right place. I'll give you exactly the treatment you want. And what's much more important, *you'll never pay a load.*

Patient: Well, Doctor, uh...

Doctor: Murray.

Patient: I beg your pardon. Is that your first name or your last name?

Doctor: Precisely!

Patient: Huh?

Doctor: My first name is Murray, and my last name is Murray. I'm Dr. Murray Murray, the no-load cardiologist! And my motto is: maybe you'll get better, maybe you won't. But you always know: *you'll never pay a load!* And these days that's the most important thing, don't you think?

Patient: Well, Doctor, I'm not sure. In fact, I think the most important thing is...not dying!

Doctor: (Smacking his forehead with delight) Ah! This is *wonderful*, sonny. I *love* a patient who knows what he wants. It makes a no-load cardiologist's job so much easier!

Patient: Well, uh, thank you, Doctor.

Doctor: My pleasure, sonny! Now, let's get right to work. First of all, what kind of treatment would you like?

Patient: What kind of treatment would I like? Doctor, shouldn't you be telling me?

Doctor: Good heavens, *no*! For that kind of cardiology, you got to pay a *load*, God forbid! In no-load cardiology, the patient picks the treatment...and I give it to him! And the most important thing is: *you never pay a load!*

Patient: Doctor, I'm just not sure I understand. Can't you give me any sort of guidance at all?

Doctor: Of course, sonny! Why didn't you ask sooner? I have this wonderful little questionnaire. I ask you questions about your symptoms, feelings, attitudes, fears, foibles and misconceptions. And when the form is all filled out, we know exactly what kind of treatment you wanted all along. And, best of all, *you never pay a load!*

Patient: Well, all right. I'll try anything. What do you want to ask me?

Doctor: Well, first of all: What's your pain tolerance?

Patient: My what?

Doctor: Your pain tolerance, sonny. How much pain do you like?

Patient: Doctor, for heaven's sake, I *hate* pain!

Doctor: See? Already we're making tremendous progress! (Makes huge, theatrical check mark on chart.) You hate pain. So already we can rule out treatments like bypass surgery, or angioplasty. Ho boy, that smarts!

Patient: (Starting to become desperate) But, Doctor, what if bypass surgery is actually the best thing for me? What if I *need* angioplasty?

Doctor: (Beaming) Sonny, rest assured: you want it, I'll perform it, same day, no questions asked! After all, I'm Dr. Murray Murray, the no-load cardiologist, and my motto is: the treatment you want is the treatment you get—with a smile! And best of all, *you'll never pay a load!*

But, my boy, you're the one who says he hates pain. So how about maybe you try some nice nitroglycerin pills. Tell me, sonny, what's your favorite flavor?

Patient: Why, uh, chocolate.

Doctor: Oh, too bad! We got no chocolate-flavored nitroglycerin pills. Got some very nice chocolate-flavored children's aspirin though. Here...

Patient: (Shouting) Wait a minute! Wait a minute! I may fall over dead of cardiac arrest at any moment, and you're giving me children's aspirin?

Doctor: Hey, sonny, now don't you get testy with me! Look here at your chart. NO PAIN, you said. CHOCOLATE, you said. Me, I've always liked licorice flavor, myself. Got some very nice licorice-flavored angina pills. But you said chocolate, so...

Patient: (Almost screaming now) Doctor! Let me make this perfectly clear! I didn't say I want chocolate. *I said I don't want to die!*

Doctor: (Sagely) And I couldn't agree with you more, sonny.

Patient: THEN WHAT EXACTLY DO YOU RECOMMEND?

Doctor: Sorry, sonny, I've tried already to explain. Recommend? This is not my field. You got the problem, you pick the treatment. (Puts arm around patient, comfortingly.) I'll be with you every step of the way. And best of all...

Patient: (miserably) Yes, yes, I know: *I'll never pay a load.* Doctor, now about these nitroglycerin pills.

Doctor: The licorice ones?

Patient: Never mind the flavor! Just tell me: do these pills have a good track record?

Doctor: Sonny! They have a *great* track record! Why, nobody who's taking these pills today is dead! Can you imagine?

Patient: What about people who stopped taking them?

Doctor: Well, sonny, you know, that's human nature. They decided they wanted 'em, then later I guess they decided they didn't want 'em anymore. May they rest in peace, sonny, but at least I can console myself: live or die, *they never pay a load.*

Patient: Oh no, not that again. Doctor, precisely what is a load?

Doctor: I couldn't really say, sonny. But it must be a terrible thing; everyone says so. Personally, I don't charge one, so I don't really know...

Patient: Didn't you go to medical school?

Doctor: (Proudly) Yes, at night, I put myself through medical school, working days as a telemarketer for a no-load mutual fund. Those were the days! We were all 20 years old, the telemarketers; not a care in the world...

Patient: (Suspiciously) What medical school did you go to?

Doctor: Dr. Bob's No-Load Cardiology and Transmission Repair Academy.

Patient: How long did you attend?

Doctor: Why, the entire four weeks!

Patient: On, my God. And when did you graduate?

Doctor: What day is this?

Patient: Thursday.

Doctor: Then it must have been…Tuesday.

Patient: This *past* Tuesday? The day before yesterday?

Doctor: Well, yes. That's the thing about no-load cardiology. It's kind of an entry-level job. Nobody stays in it for very long, because it doesn't pay much. How could it? It's no-load.

Patient: I think I'm starting to feel faint…

Doctor: Not to worry, sonny. I won't abandon you. I'm Dr. Murray Murray, the no-load cardiologist. And my motto is: I may not know much, but my heart's in the right place. *Your* heart, on the other hand…

Patient: Doctor, that isn't funny!

Doctor: Oh, excuse me, sonny! I read somewhere that humor is therapeutic.

Patient: In a medical journal?

Doctor: I think it was in *Reader's Digest.*

Patient: I think this is a case of the blind leading the blind!

Doctor: Maybe so, sonny, but you got to admit: the price is right.

Patient: Actually, I'm starting to wonder.

Doctor: You lost me, sonny.

Patient: Not yet, Doctor, but I'm working on it. What I meant was: I'm starting to realize that I don't just need treatment, *I need sound professional advice.* Even if I have to pay for it.

Doctor: You know, sonny, I could use some professional advice myself.

Patient: Why?

Doctor: Well, I've been getting these pains in my chest.

Patient: You, Doctor? Well, what are you taking for it?

Doctor: Reese's Pieces.

Patient: Reese's Pieces?

Doctor: Yes. They always made E.T. feel better, so...

Patient: Are they working?

Doctor: Well, no...but since I prescribed them for myself...

Patient: Yes, I know: at least you didn't pay a load. Doc, I think you better get your hat, and let's both go see a full-service cardiologist.

Doctor: I don't know, sonny. I read a detailed study that said you're *never* supposed to do that.

Patient: Was that in a medical journal?

Doctor: No, it was in the same issue of *Reader's Digest.* It's the only one I own.

Patient: But doctors don't write *Reader's Digest.*

Doctor: No, journalists do; you think that's part of the problem?

Patient: I don't know; it's not my field. Are you coming, Doc?

Doctor: (Sadly, putting on his battered porkpie hat.) I guess so.

(Doctor and patient exit stage right, past a desk in the outer office, where the nurse is intently reading something.)

Doctor: My patient and I are going out for the afternoon.

Nurse: Fine, Doctor; where shall I forward your calls?

Doctor: I'd rather not say. Say, is that *Reader's Digest* you've got there?

Nurse: Why no, Doctor, it's the *Journal of the American Medical Association.* I'm studying to be a neurosurgeon.

Doctor: Not a no-load neurosurgeon?

Nurse: Never!

Doctor: (Forlornly, to patient) A very bright woman. Smarter than I, in some ways. She'll go far...

(Doctor and patient exit. The skeleton falls over on its face. The doctor's diploma falls off the wall. The curtain falls.)

The Pernicious Fiction
Of Track Record

*This is the article that got me mugged by **The Wall
Street Journal.***

*You see, journalism has completely bought into the
no-load myth: (a) picking a superior fund is the critical
issue; (b) past performance is the key determinant of a
superior fund; (c) by following past performance, you
can pick superior funds no-load, because you don't
really need help just to pick a fund.*

*For reasons impossible to imagine, **The Wall Street
Journal** decided to run an article suggesting that
brokers don't want their clients to be "savvy," i.e. to
know a fund's track record. As proof of this the **Journal**
reporter cited two sentences from this column.*

The only things wrong with this were:

(1) She quoted me out of context.

*(2) The fact that she was quoting from a written piece
was deliberately obscured, creating the false impression
that I'd said these things to the reporter (or someone).*

*(3) The reporter didn't speak to me before the
publication of the article, nor did she attempt to do so
in any serious way.*

*(4) When the reporter's editor asked if she had
spoken to me, the reporter (as the editor later
acknowledged to me) misled the editor into thinking
that she had.*

*Apprised of this personal outrage, the editor
conceded to me that the paper had acted wrongly, and
invited me to write a letter stating my position. Need I
tell you that the letter was never published? (Need I
explain to you why **Absence of Malice** has always
been one of my favorite movies?)*

*That's my story, and I'm sticking to it. The article
itself is self-explanatory. My core belief is stated in the
article, in capital letters:*

*"TRACK RECORD, MORE RELIABLY
THAN ANY OTHER SINGLE VARIABLE,
SETS THE INVESTOR UP TO FAIL."*

Now let me tell you why...

November, 1993

The Pernicious Fiction Of Track Record

A couple of months ago I suggested in this space that you stop selling track record (*Getting Ready For The Fall*, September 1993). On its best day, track record only serves to make fearful investors greedy (and greedy investors even greedier). And, after a decade of spectacular bull markets in both bonds and stocks, fostering greed may make you some sales, but—probably sooner than later—it'll lose you a lot of clients.

This month, I'd like to expand on this point—which is to say, I'd like to dump even harder and more loudly on track-record selling. Readers of my book *Serious Money: The Art Of Marketing Mutual Funds* know that I've always regarded track record as an excruciatingly dumb, weak way to sell money management.

Today, I feel even more strongly about track record being the wrong way to sell mutual funds. Low interest rates continue to turn us from a nation of savers into—albeit unwillingly, and perhaps even unwittingly—a nation of investors. And track-record selling is no longer merely dumb. It's downright **evil.**

Dumb, Dumb, Dumb

Let's review the dumb aspects of track-record selling. Then, as we go along, you'll start to see the dumbness sliding over into the evil zone. Watch carefully; it doesn't happen all at once.

1. The Dumbest Thing About Track-Record Selling Is That It Renders You Superfluous. Or rather, you render yourself superfluous. The more your presentations make track record a critical (much less *the* critical) variable, the more clearly you tell the investor to just go buy *Money* magazine's top-performing no-load fund.

So, when you say, "My fund did 18.26% over the last ten years, and (fill in the blank) only did 18.16%," the prospect nods sagely, leafs through as many magazines as it takes for him to find a no-load fund that did 18.27%—and then, adios muchacho. (Which is Spanish for: I hope you and all other salesmen of load funds freeze to death in the dark.) In other words, by suggesting that the key variable is one which is readily available from any one of a dozen or more magazines or newspapers, you render yourself superfluous.

You ensure that doesn't happen by saying, "My advice is the critical variable. Track record, like any other number, takes you just so far and no further. And where it takes you ain't *nearly* far enough. **I take you the rest of the way,** to where you need to be."

2. Track Record Selling Suggests That The Critical Variables In Successful Investing Are Measurable And, Therefore, Objectively Knowable. But of course, they're not. If there were a reliably consistent system for successful investing, somebody (or, more accurately, somebody's computer) would already have figured out what it is, and would have long since cleaned out everybody else in the game.

That hasn't happened. In fact, the overwhelming majority of equity fund managers—armed with a limitless supply of the best research available—fail to outperform the Standard & Poor's 500-Stock Index. Which tells you that, whatever "it" is, "it" isn't knowable. Track-record selling says "it" is track record...and track record is knowable.

Crossing The Line

It's at this point, then, that track-record selling begins crossing the line from being merely dumb (see point #1, above) to becoming marginally evil. Why? Because track-record selling encourages the investor's worst instincts. Faced with the intensely anxiety-producing task of investing, investors will usually exhibit a deep psychic need "for two and two always to make four."

But it doesn't. In investing (as in baseball, and life), nothing works all the time. Two and two may very often make four, but occasionally it'll make five. And, once in a great while, it'll make fish. (The great Zen master Charles Dillon Stengel expressed this ambiguity perfectly when he observed, "Good pitching always beats good hitting. And vice versa.")

A very successful financial planner of my acquaintance says that his most successful clients, as a class, are widows. That's because their husbands told them to trust my acquaintance, and they do. So they leave him alone and, of course, he does very well for them.

This planner's least successful investors are engineers. Because, out of their deep, sick need for two and two to make four, they're always trying to outthink his advice. So they always grab the controls and drill the plane right into the side of a mountain.

Track record (or expense ratios, or the number of Morningstar stars, or any other single "objective" measurement) will thus always set up the investor to destroy himself. And will, therefore, be not merely dumb, but at least a little bit evil.

3. Track Record Totally Ignores The Issue Of Risk. Dumb, and increasingly evil. Dumb because it implicitly suggests that investing is a one-variable equation, when, in fact, there are very few, if any, one-variable equations. The return produced by a manager is, no doubt, interesting. However, it's not really meaningful unless you understand the risk the manager took to achieve that return.

Neil Eigen, director of equity investing at Bear Stearns Asset Management, once said to me that *any* money manager could be in the top 1% of all equity managers—**provided he was willing to risk being in the bottom 1%.** In other words, anybody can bet his fund so heavily on one thesis that, if that thesis is right, his numbers will blow everybody else's away. If his thesis *doesn't* come home, of course, he'll be a total non-starter. And the investor will never catch up.

So, while the track-record investor may be thrilled to discover, with the aid of the track-record salesperson, a big-cap value fund that's done 23% over the last five years, he won't notice that the manager bet 40% of the portfolio on oil stocks, let's say, and oil went from $15 to $24 per barrel. But, what if oil had gone back to $10 per barrel? And even if oil prices soared, what does the manager do for an encore? These, and many other important questions, are begged by overemphasizing track record.

Incidentally, while we're on the subject of things to which track record blinds you, let's not forget the increasingly important issue of taxes. Track record is, of course, a pre-tax number. But, depending on a manager's turnover style, the *taxability* of the return may skew after-tax returns all over the map.

4. Today's Track Records May Very Well Be Unrepeatable. It is, I suppose, technically possible that the bond market will produce the same sort of returns over the next ten years as it did over the last ten. (It's also at least technically possible that I'll get elected Pope.) But, unless you think the long Treasury bond is going to 2%, to quote a long-term bond fund's ten-year track record with a straight face is, I believe, to actively and knowingly mislead your prospect. This is only a little dumb; mostly, it's evil.

Indeed, the rally in the bond market has been so spectacular that the ten-year return of bond funds (about 14% to 15%) is fairly close to the ten-year return of stocks (18% to 19%). So, if you just went on ten-year track record, you'd have to be nuts to take the added risk of stocks.

Thus, we've now arrived at the point where track record, while it may be factually correct, leads you to conclude the opposite of the truth. Namely, that the return from bonds isn't all that much less than the return from stocks.

But, of course, the truth is that, over the long term, stocks have returned about twice what bonds have. On Mark Twain's list of the three kinds of lies—lies, damned lies and statistics—I, therefore, submit that bond funds' ten-year record is solidly in the third category.

The issues are somewhat less black and white in stock funds, I think. (Stocks' ten-year returns have only been around twice their Ibbotson trendline return, while bonds have done pretty close to three times theirs.) Still, the investor is likely to react even more emotionally to disappointments in stocks—because he probably felt so much shakier about them going in. So beware of citing the record; it's accurate, but it may still be misleading.

5. An Individual Fund's Track Record May Not Be Repeatable. The returns on an *investment* are not usually related to the returns of the *investor*...because, reading track record ads in the newspaper, the investor piles in after the record has been established.

Maybe it's the fund's size that will do it in. It's one thing to compile a great record in a small-cap/emerging-growth fund while the fund goes from zero to $100 million in assets. But when, on the basis of the record, the fund gets to $1.2 billion, look out below. How can it buy enough stock in a nifty little company to make a difference any more? And, even if it can...how does it sell?

6. Every Manager's Style Will Sometimes Go Completely Out Of Sync With The Market, Usually When He's Got The Best Record In Town. In the value stock/mergers and acquisitions market of the '80s, Mario Gabelli became king of the hill. His record was all the more brilliant for being so consistent—10-year, 5-year, 3-year; you name it, he ranked right up there with the best of the best. At that point, a major brokerage firm raised about $1.1 billion for a Gabelli open-end fund in a couple of months.

Immediately, we had the M & A cardiac arrest/value is dead/mini-crash of Friday, October 13, 1989. Growth was king; value was yesterday's news. Gabelli, God bless him, stuck firmly to his style, looking neither to the right nor to the left—and "underperformed," for a while. As a result, by the Spring of '92, that open-end fund's assets were down to about $530 million, and *Forbes* and others wondered in print if Mario hadn't lost his touch.

Today, **every single thing** Gabelli was betting on (value/telecommunications/M&A) is busting out all over. And once again we hear the cry: Mario for mayor. The lesson: you don't buy a great manager when his record is a beacon unto the masses. You buy him when he's in the doghouse. Once again, track record sends *exactly* the wrong signal.

This is true not just of individual managers, but of styles (growth vs. value, big cap vs. small cap) as well. And it's truest—with a particular vengeance—about sectors. At the end of 1991, if we went on track record, we'd have put 100% of our new money in health-care funds and 0% in REITs, right?

Am I getting through to you on this? TRACK RECORD, MORE RELIABLY THAN ANY OTHER SINGLE VARIABLE, SETS THE INVESTOR UP TO FAIL. Track-record selling, therefore, isn't just dumb. IT'S DOWNRIGHT EVIL.

I rest my case.

The Better Message

If track-record selling is at the very least dumb and at the very worst evil, what should you be telling prospects to foster the long-term act of faith, without which there can be no real investment success? When your prospect asks, "Why buy this fund?," you should answer:

1. Because I Own It. If you want to be a 300% better, more effective salesperson/communicator, make it a principle to buy what you're selling.

Your average client will never know 1% of what you know about money management. So, if he trusts you, why doesn't he just buy the fund(s) you and your family have staked your future on? And if he doesn't trust you, what's the basis for your relationship?

2. Because This Fund Company Will Always Be There. Face it, boys and girls: with 4300 funds out there (1000 of which are less than a year old), there are way, **way** too many funds and fund companies.

You can slice a salami only so thin. With or without benefit of a major, long-lasting bear market (which a startling percentage of today's money managers have never actually seen), my guess is that a quarter to a third of these entities need to disappear.

Do you want to explain that to your clients? Neither do I. Today more than ever, I'll cheerfully give up a few basis points of track record—and maybe more than a few—to get size, stability and longevity.

3. Because They've Been Managing Money For A Long, Long Time, And There Isn't Much—If Anything—They Haven't Seen. If a fund company was managing money before the '29 Crash and all the way through the Great Depression...what disaster can your client foresee that the company hasn't not only survived, but thrived on?

Does somebody new have a better "track record"? I don't doubt it. And I don't care. Professor John Kenneth Galbraith (who isn't usually right) very wisely observed, "Financial genius is a short memory in a rising market." And President Truman (who was almost always right) said, "The only new thing in the world is the history you don't know." Is it possible that a good measure of *real* track record might be the number of the manager's grey hairs and bullet holes?

4. They Manage An Awful Lot Of Money For Some Very Big, Very Smart Investors. When you're showing a manager who's running $40 billion (some in mutual funds, but some in $10 million minimum separate accounts for Yale, or GM, or the Chicago Police Department), that, in and of itself, is part of the "record."

Every money manager in America is pitching Yale's account. And Yale, to put it mildly, can tell the difference between chicken salad and chicken...uh, feathers. It does not seem to bother Yale if its managers don't happen to be on *Money* magazine's top-40 pick-hits-of-the-week. "So why should it bother you, Mr. Client?"

And the last, loveliest and most pertinent (in the context of this article) reason your client should love this fund/manager?

5. Because, Over The Last Five Years, He's Had A Mediocre Track Record. He has a consistent, well-thought-out discipline/strategy. He's stuck to that approach, allowing the smart investor to dollar-cost average, even while it's been out of vogue. Money has been flowing *out* of the fund. No matter which magazine's top-ten list you look at, this fund ain't on it. Journalists don't interview the manager any more.

What more evidence can you possibly ask for that, on the next turn of the wheel, **this fund is going to shoot out every light in the joint**?

* * * * * *

Hide behind anything—a track-record number, a chart, any piece of paper—and you not only cheapen yourself, you ultimately misinform the investor.

Make yourself indispensable—your experience, your judgment, your ability to see what isn't immediately obvious—and you ennoble your role, earn your compensation, and make the client a better investor than he could possibly be without you.

We've Only Just Begun

Reacting (though not, I hope, overreacting) to the notoriety generated by the "Getting Ready For The Fall" piece, I returned to my traditional year-end-raging-long-term-bull format as the curtain came down on 1993.

*People really seemed to like the quote from Michael Rothschild's book **Bionomics: The Inevitability of Capitalism,** where he compresses the history of our species into the equivalent of a 24-hour day. The resultant notion—how recent real progress is, and how fast it's accelerating— was (and is) really a grabber.*

***Bionomics** and the other book featured in this article, Charles R. Morris's **The Coming Global Boom,** are required reading for the 21st Century asset gatherer.*

But until you can get to these...

December, 1993

We've Only Just Begun

In September's column, "Getting Ready For The Fall" (written in August, the month the long bond hit 5.79%), I suggested that the nirvana-like state we'd been living in all year was likely to be coming to an abrupt and painful end.

I was particularly convinced that the debt markets erroneously thought the economic recovery was Clark Kent. I, on the other hand, was virtually certain that the recovery was Superman. So, when the economy dove into the phone booth and came out with a one-month, eight-tenths of one percent jump in industrial production, the bond market went into traumatic shock.

By Thanksgiving, the long bond had backed up to 6.4%, devastating not only the bond market but also all manner of interest-rate-sensitive stocks, most notably utilities and real estate investment trusts.

So, I was actually feeling pretty good. There are, after all, only two kinds of people in the world: people with too much class to say "I told you so," and people like me. So you can imagine what a deeply religious experience it was for me to be asked by a wirehouse sales executive, "Hey, are you still bearish on the market?"

I asked him to re-read the article because I was never "bearish on the market." I'd taken pains to make clear that, while I thought we were way overdue for some kind of short- to intermediate-term correction, I remained a raging, table-pounding, long-term bull.

Why I'm A Long-Term Bull

In this final column of the year, then, let me return to—and offer some new perspectives on—the exact nature of my long-term bullishness.

1. *With age comes a longer-term perspective. And with long-term perspective comes the realization that optimism is simply the only realism.* The older you get, the more apocalypses du jour you see evanescing, like dewdrops on an August morning.

I celebrated my 50th birthday on October 11th. So, I missed the Mother of All Evanescent Apocalypses Du Jour, the so-called Great Depression. But there've been lots more, and indeed, I was born smack in the middle of the next one. It was called World War II.

On the day of my birth, October 11, 1943, the temperature never got above 60 degrees in Gotham. Joe McCarthy's New York Yankees won the World Series over the St. Louis Cardinals on a home run by catcher Bill Dickey—who died just last month. The Dow Jones Industrial Average closed at 136.61, on NYSE volume of 479,583 shares. (Most days in 1993, three NYSE stocks each traded more shares than that.)

And, by October 11, 1943, you knew the good guys were going to win the war. Oddly enough, that was, economically and financially, the bad news.

By that time, both of our enemies had taken their best shots, and failed. The Japanese were doomed after Coral Sea and Midway; Hitler was well along the road to ruin after turning from the English Channel and inexplicably invading Russia. It would take a while, and the cost in blood and treasure would be awful, but you knew we were going to win. And when we won, we'd surely go right back into the Depression.

It was, everyone assumed, only the war that had finally pulled us out of the Depression. Without the artificial stimulus of war spending—and especially when millions of GIs came home to no jobs—the end of the war would surely mean economic disaster.

Of course, it didn't work out that way. And that's the story of my life...and everyone's life, really.

Later, during the week of my 30th birthday, in 1973, I watched the price of oil triple overnight and the vice president of the U.S. resign in disgrace to avoid imprisonment...all in seven days' time. Surely that double-whammy economic/constitutional apocalypse du jour would put us under! No such luck.

Berlin, Korea, the Cuban missile crisis, assassinations, Vietnam, Watergate, Yamani (or ya life), hyperinflation, junk bonds, October 19, Saddam, Perot...apocalypses du jour turn out to be a lot like the crosstown bus: if you missed the last one, just hang out, there'll be another along in a few minutes.

And, in the long run, that one won't matter, either. Because, when the apocalypse du jour collides with the genius of democratic capitalism, the good guys always win.

2. *People always assume that progress is linear, if not actually over; in fact, progress is always exponential.* It is always fashionable to assume that problems are exponential and solutions linear or non-existent. Human ingenuity—the sheer volume of new ideas waiting to be thought of—constantly surprises us, because we always underestimate it.

Thomas Malthus declared in 1798 that population growth was exponential, but "the power of the earth to provide subsistence" finite; he foresaw "a gigantic, inevitable famine" (and, in so doing, earned economics its nickname, "the dismal science").

Of course, food production has outstripped population growth from that day to this. Malthus, as George Gilder recently wrote, "failed to grasp that it is not the earth but man that produces food." Human ingenuity, from John Deere's first plow to today's giant combines, has forced the real cost of food down relentlessly. In the U.S. today, the cost of food as a percentage of the average household budget is at its lowest point ever—and continuing to decline steadily. And wait 'til biotech really kicks in.

It's progress, not problems, that moves exponentially. Since the dawn of human consciousness, man dreamed of flying. The Wright brothers finally did it—and within the span of one human lifetime, there was a man standing on the moon.

Johann Gutenberg had all the bugs out of movable metal type by the spring of 1454. Over the next 18 months, he produced 200 bibles, all exactly the same. Everybody thought that's what the new invention was for: bibles, maybe dictionaries, stuff like that. A few big books for a few rich guys.

Just 45 years later, in 1500, 1,000 presses in Europe turned out ten million copies of 35,000 different titles. Exponential growth of knowledge was already leading to exponential progress, and the potential for universal education was just around the corner.

3. *Progress, in a very real sense, is just getting started.* As Michael Rothschild points out in his brilliant book, **Bionomics: The Inevitability of Capitalism**, our species—called homo sapiens sapiens —has been walking around for about 100,000 years. Compress that into a 24-hour day and the story of our species goes like this: From midnight until 10 p.m., we're hunter/gatherers. From 10 p.m. until 11:57 p.m., we're subsistence farmers and craftspeople. The modern industrial age, which Rothschild dates from Watt's steam engine in 1775, is three minutes old.

And the microprocessor—the entire computer on a microchip, the single greatest human technological breakthrough—was invented 19 seconds ago, in 1971.

The microprocessor has already made possible simultaneous revolutions is the workplace (personal computers, word processors, handheld calculators that cost $30 and have more computing power than ENIAC—the first "mainframe" computer—had in 1947), entertainment (VCRs, camcorders, video games), medicine (magnetic resonance imaging), communications (cellular phones) and a host of other areas, from supermarket scanners and bank ATMs to electronic fuel injection and anti-lock brakes.

Indeed, microchip technology is now merging with fiber optics to create a new information economy. Gilder predicts that "the technologies of computers and communications will each advance roughly a millionfold in cost effectiveness in the next ten years." Small wonder that Sir John Templeton recently said, "It has often taken 1,000 years for the standard of living to double in the most advanced countries, yet it may double for the world as a whole in the next 20 years."

Finally, today's technological advances not only don't eliminate jobs, net-net they create jobs...and they're environmentally benign, in the bargain.

Gilder points out that during the past 30 years, the U.S. has led the world both in technology and in jobs. "Deploying three times as much computer power per capita as Japan or Europe, the U.S. has created some 35 million new jobs. Automation is its own remedy—

by creating wealth, technology endows new work."

And, as our progress becomes more information intensive, it becomes more energy efficient. Microchips are, after all, made of the three most common elements in the earth's crust—silicon, aluminum and oxygen.

4. *Oh, yeah? Well, what about the deficit?* What deficit? Charles R. Morris, in his great book **The Coming Global Boom**, points out several oddities in government accounting which tend to make the deficit look worse than it is.

One glaring instance is that we take as current expenses the costs of infrastructure improvements (bridges, tunnels, highways), rather than capitalizing them and writing them off over their useful lives— and against their stream of future revenues.

Moreover, Morris points out, if the U.S. spent the same percentage of its GNP on defense as do our NATO allies, we would have no deficit. (And what will happen when all the brain power that goes into the black hole of defense is turned loose on the private sector?)

Incidentally, how come you've heard of (and maybe even read) Figgie's *Bankruptcy 1995* but never heard of Rothschild's and Morris' books? (You'll be charmed to learn, incidentally, that in Canada they have a book—also a big bestseller—making almost the same arguments as Figgie; it's called *The Great Reckoning*. They never heard of Rothschild and Morris either.)

Could it be that you, too, have fallen for the lunatic notion that problems are exponential and human ingenuity finite, when all your life experience tells you it's the other way around? Long-term bearishness is, after all, literally counterintuitive: it's the supposition that the exact opposite of everything you've ever experienced is going to happen.

5. *When those wonderful folks who brought you the Tienanmen Square massacre are now urging all their countrymen to get rich, you have to know that something new—and profoundly bullish—is going on in the world.* 'Nuff said?

Back To The Beginning

What on earth has all this got to do with "Sales & Marketing"—

145

the alleged subject of this monthly column? Only everything, that's all.

You see, I believe that, in the end, people don't buy what you know. They buy what you believe. And the long-term bullishness (which, again, I regard merely as cold realism) recited above is the core of my belief system.

Investors want, need and deserve to be constantly reminded that, in the long run, it's not just going to be all right, it's going to be terrific. Faith in the future is the essence of becoming an investor. (Want to see investment in this country triple overnight? Phase out FDIC insurance. Please.)

Investors, like all other human beings, want to be led (not managed; it's not the same thing). Want to be a leader of investors? Put a solid, rational, logical and unshakeable faith in the future at the core of your belief system. And you'll do business—especially in bad markets—on a scale you never dreamed possible.

And that's my wish for every reader of this column, in 1994 and beyond.

A Rose Is Not A Rose

The IAFP invited me to give an address to their
1993 Convention in Dallas, but asked that I
create a new presentation that the attendees
would not have heard me do before. Since I had
been doing some reading in the field of
linguistics and communication, it occurred to me
to explore a phenomenon I've observed all my
career—that there are quite a few critically
important words and phrases in our professional
lexicon that have wildly different meanings to us
and our clients.

The resulting presentation was a pretty big hit
at the Convention, so I decided to excerpt it for
my first column of 1994. Re-reading it now, I see
a summary point I should have made (but
didn't). Namely, that if you're talking like most of
the other reps are talking, it's a sign that you're
thinking the way most other reps are
thinking...which probably means you're going to
get the same results most other reps are
getting...which are, almost by
definition, mediocre.

That's why I recommend that you tape
yourself extensively for a month or so, allowing
you to really hear the way you express yourself.
This can be very scary, but very therapeutic.

Think about this, as you read how "a rose is
not a rose"...

A Rose Is
Not A Rose

In the seminal work on communication by Dr. Albert Mehrabian, it was discovered that most of what we register in any conversation is non-verbal. And very nearly everything else is verbal nuance: the way we say what we say, rather than what we say. (Mehrabian and the other people in white coats call this latter phenomenon "paralinguistics.") Words themselves, it turns out, are only a tiny fraction of total communication.

In sales, this communications pyramid is turned upside down, so that words are the "point" upon which the fragile balance of real communication rests. So to me (using Mehrabian's exact percentages of the three elements of communication), the pyramid looks like below.

Do you see my "point"? The balance of the pyramid (and of your interview) may be irreparably upset by very small miscommunications about certain key words and phrases.

Keeping The Pyramid Upright

The words I want to discuss are particularly notable for the fact that, while their meaning to us is precise and intellectual, their con-

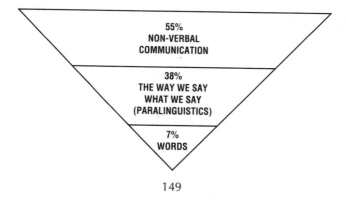

55%
NON-VERBAL
COMMUNICATION

38%
THE WAY WE SAY
WHAT WE SAY
(PARALINGUISTICS)

7%
WORDS

notations to the client/prospect are extremely imprecise and very, very emotional. And, since we know that investors make their decisions based on their emotions, this is a very important "point." If we unwittingly upset an investor emotionally (without ever realizing that we've done so, because the word that set him off is so innocuous to us), the whole interview can topple over—on us.

Moreover, since our personality type gets highly nervous in a sales interview—we're keyed up, we're high achievers, we've got a big emotional investment in winning—we tend to pay much too much attention to what we're saying. Instead, we should be putting our energy into watching how the prospect is reacting to what we're saying. But we can't—so we don't hear the pyramid rumbling as it starts to tip over, while there's still time to right it.

So I suggest that, as you speak to clients and prospects, you try to visualize that inverted pyramid. And ask yourself constantly, "Is it remaining in good balance? Am I saying any word that's likely to detonate an emotional charge and topple it over?"

Words And Phrases To Watch Out For

Here's a bouquet of these words and phrases, each of which we use intellectually and conceptually, but which the client receives emotionally—and which may set off tectonically deep and destabilizing resonances.

1. Risk—A recurrent theme in this column since I began writing it in 1990 has been that Americans see risk as only one thing: loss of principal. But the great financial risk for most of us is the inexorable erosion of our purchasing power. As we retire much sooner and live much longer, even very low levels of inflation will grind our dollars into powder over time.

So, when you so much as say the word "risk" (or respond in kind to your prospect's use of the word "risk" as he understands it), you may find yourself suddenly (albeit metaphorically) unable to breathe. That's because the pyramid has toppled completely over, and has come to rest on your chest. Game over.

For instance, suppose the prospect said, "But what about the risk of the stock market?" You might (with perfect intellectual correctness) have cheerfully replied, "Time leaches all the risk out of the stock market." The good news is you're right; the bad news is you're dead.

Because you accepted the definition of "risk" of your Depression-ravaged, principal-obsessed prospect, you confirmed his prejudices, which dictate that the real way you manage risk is to stay the hell out of stocks in the first place!

The correct answer, of course, was, "I'm not sure I know what you mean. How are you defining the risk of the stock market?" He says, "losing my money." You say, in wonderment, "But how on earth can anyone do that? Sixty-odd years ago, the Dow Jones Industrial Average was 40. The other day it was at 3850. How do you lose money in something that does that? And what about (here you hand him an EXPO '74 ten-cent postage stamp, laminated to your business card) *the real risk* in your and your wife's life?"

In this way, you regain control over the agenda, so that the pyramid stops whipping around in the wind like the Sears Tower and you can safely proceed with the interview.

2. Safety—Same as "risk," only in reverse. When the prospect says, "I've got to keep my money safe," you don't start arguing that stocks (or even bonds, for that matter) are safe *long term*. That just confirms that real safety is staying in CDs. You ask, "Safe from what?" Or, "How are you defining safety?" Or (holding up your EXPO '74 stamp), "Safe from which financial risk?" Or, if you're feeling very brave, "Well, safety, to me, is preserving what your money will buy. Certainty, on the other hand, is preserving the number of paper dollars you own. Are you talking about *safety or certainty?*"

Safety is not avoiding risk. You can't avoid risk. If you accept the very small risk of owning shares of great businesses (a risk which, over any historical 15-year period since 1926, is zero), you avoid the very real risk of having to ask your children for money in your old age. As soon as my prospect and I agree on that, the pyramid stops wobbling!

3. Growth—A truly terrible word, growth is always taken by the investor (unconsciously) as the antithesis of income. And Americans virtually all invest for income—even when they don't spend the income. (Look at the staggering percentage of bond fund dividends that are reinvested.) Ask the prospect to invest for "growth," and you're quite literally asking him to go against all his deepest psychic/financial needs.

Besides, nobody alive is investing for "growth" as an end in itself. All investments are made for the production of an income some day. If I'm 65, I'm investing for the production of an income tomorrow. If I'm 45, I'm investing for the production of an income in 15 or 20 years. We're all income investors; it's just that we all have different time horizons for the onset of that income. Growth? What's that? (My sister-in-law had a growth once, but the doctors found it in time.)

The notion of "growth" cuts the investor off emotionally from everything he feels comfortable with. So, instead of talking about the "growth potential" of owning great businesses, talk about their "peerless record of producing a rising stream of dividends."

Businesses, you see, always share increased profits with their owners, but never share them with their lenders. No business ever came back to its 30-year bondholders after ten years and said, "Hey, guys, we're making so much more money than we thought we ever would that we're raising the coupon on your bond." Instead, they gave the extra earnings (above and beyond what they reinvested in the business) to the owners, in the form of increased dividends.

Growth of capital is a hopeless abstraction, but growth of income is something everyone can relate to. If your prospect needs a little prompting, just show him your EXPO '74 ten-cent stamp. "Let's say you retired in 1974, Mr. Jones, and all you needed to buy every year was one first-class postage stamp. So you lent your capital to AT&T, General Electric, Pfizer and Coca-Cola. And they paid you twenty cents in interest. Since a stamp only costs ten cents, you'd have felt pretty good.

"Today, in 1994, (a) you're still here, (b) those great companies are still paying you twenty cents (or less, actually, because interest rates have gone way down since '74), and (c) a stamp costs 29 cents. **Lend** to great companies, and they'll never pay you a penny more (or less) than they promised. **Own** those great companies, and the income stream you'll receive will rise faster—sometimes much faster—than your living costs."

The sign over James Carville's desk when he managed the Clinton presidential campaign read, "It's the economy, stupid." If you insist on talking about "growth" at all, put a sign over your own desk to remind you: "It's growth of income, stupid."

Which brings us, of course, to:

4. Income—As in, when you're talking about the great companies to a nervous saver/investor, "But what if I need income?"

The traditional concept of income among American savers and investors is fatally flawed (and therefore instantly capable of toppling the pyramid if left unchecked) in two ways. It's fixed. And it's nominal.

Income from a bond is different from, and better than, income from a stock—at least in your prospect's mind. (It's also—and this is really dangerous—higher. A 6% bond pays more than a great company's stock yielding 3%. Are you starting to be able to hear that rumbling sound?)

To stop the pyramid from swaying at the mere sound of the word "income," you have to unfix the connotation. I always use the Wayne Gretzky quote to establish this point: "Most people skate to where the puck is. I skate to where it's going to be." Don't tell me where yields are *now*. Everybody knows where yields are *now*, and there's no way to make money merely knowing what everyone else knows. Ask yourself: where are yields *going to be* five, ten, fifteen and twenty years from now.

Don't know? Fine; neither do I, so let's concentrate on what we do know: bond coupons never get raised until the bond matures; cash dividends from great companies always get raised. So, 6% may be more income now, but 3% will be more income later. If it sounds to you like I'm recycling the point I just made (it's growth of income, stupid), you bet I am, and with a vengeance!

I would cheerfully invest entirely in fixed-income investments for the rest of my life if someone would only fix my living costs. Since no one will, I regard the term "fixed income" as being on an oxymoronic par with the phrase "water landing." There just ain't no such thing. If the dollar of income I'm getting is the same, my real income (in other words, my purchasing power) is falling all the bloody time. Which is why the other potentially destabilizing fiction built into the common usage of the word "income" is that you can look at it in nominal terms.

You actually meet people these days who are waiting for interest rates to go back up! Such is the hypnotic power of nominal rates. Does anyone really believe that when the long bond is 8% instead of 6%, his purchasing power will have gone up by a third? He'll be lucky if after the higher tax rates and the resurgence of inflation that it'd take to get you from 6% to 8%, his real income hasn't fallen by one-third!

Finally, the thing I hate most about the term "income" is that it's emotionally cut off from the concept of "principal." They're two separate things, in the popular conception; money somehow isn't fungible.

If you're retiring today at 60, and you absolutely need 7% "income" from your investments, the traditional concept of income and principal as separate entities is just going to flat kill you...and sooner than later.

You see, to get 7% from a bond portfolio, you'll have to build one hellaciously risky bond portfolio, won't you? Moreover, ten years from now, when that fixed income is worth a third less in terms of purchasing power, you're going to be in real trouble.

If somebody had just warned you off the concept of "income," reminding you that all money is fungible, you might have set up a systematic withdrawal plan from a nice, cozy equity income fund.

You'd take the 3% current dividend, draw down the other 4% in principal, sit back and relax, knowing two things. First, your income's going to go up nearly every year, as the great companies raise their dividends. Second, since a good equity income fund has probably been doing 8% to 9% this last half century, chances are that not only is your current income rising, but your principal's accreting as well.

Now, how do you define "income," again?

5. Stocks and

6. The Stock Market—To you and me, a stock is an ownership interest in a great business; to the folks we talk to, it's a casino chip. And most folks don't go to casinos with their serious money. (This also explains why I never, ever, say the phrase blue chip. Am I getting through to you on this?)

Likewise, we use the phrase "the stock market" to express the concept "the sum of all equities." The folks receive the phrase emotionally as "casino where the odds are just naturally against you."

The critical issue is that the great American saver and investor has no concept that stocks are companies. A recent *Wall Street Journal* article about investors who were getting sandbagged in utility funds quoted a guy who said he might sell before his fund went, and I quote, "down the tubes." (I guess the *Journal* staffer was too busy reporting the news to stop and tell this poor guy the truth—but then truth and news have never been closely related concepts.)

Where'd he think Texas Utilities, Penn Power & Light, the Southern Company and Boston Edison were going? The answer is he didn't know; he didn't realize that stocks are companies.

Don't say stocks, say "companies" or "businesses," interchangeably. And, for the stock market, say "the market for the shares of the better businesses in America."

7. Aggressive and

8. Conservative—These are just other incarnations of "risk" and "safety"—only worse, because they're judgmental. Here's what I mean by that. A forty-year-old couple has roughly four decades of rising prices to deal with. They can dollar-cost-average for at least the next 20 years.

Is a small-cap growth fund in any meaningful sense too aggressive for these folks? It's just the opposite, for two reasons. First, small-cap stocks historically produce a 20% higher return than big-cap. (It's just common sense: without the premium return, who'd take the added risk?) So, since these folks are trying to conserve (and accrete) purchasing power—net of inflation and taxes—small-cap is 20% more likely to accomplish their goal. In some very real sense, then, for this couple, small-cap is more conservative.

Moreover, since our two friends are going to dollar-cost-average, they'll obviously do better (in other words, make more money) in something that has higher highs and lower lows. (If you don't immediately grasp this, read the appendix on dollar cost averaging in my book "Serious Money.") The more they make, the more they're achieving their goal of conserving/accreting purchasing power...and therefore the more "conservative" small-cap is for them.

The point here is that "aggressive" and "conservative" aren't absolute terms, nor ought they to be related solely to an investment. They're relative terms, which only take on real meaning when related to the potential investor.

Put another way, suppose these same 40-year-olds started buying two-year Treasury bonds. Very conservative, right? Of course not. Two-year Treasury bonds, net of inflation and taxes, are depleting their purchasing power, because they have a negative real return. It's the financial equivalent of high blood pressure: painless, no external symptoms at all...and, with every beat of their hearts, it's killing them. "Conservative?" No; the ultimate recklessness...for them.

Keep your eye on that pyramid.

There's No Such Thing As No Risk

This was a sequel to, and an extension of, "A Rose Is Not A Rose." I got a lot of comments on it; people really seemed to love the analogy of "full" and "empty" gasoline drums. Just as the gasoline drum is never "empty" of danger, no investment is ever "empty" of risk...it's just full of a different risk, the way the gasoline drum is full of another danger. "Money is always at risk," I wrote, and went on to examine "the toxicity of groupthink."

There's No Such Thing As No Risk

Last month, in "A Rose Is Not A Rose," I pointed out that certain words and phrases have radically different meanings for us and our prospects, and how our sales conversations can get short-circuited by the careless use of those words.

Since working on that piece (it was originally a speech I gave at last September's IAFP convention), I've done some more reading in the field of linguistics. And I've found some things that may help you better understand the way in which language can distort thought.

For example, here's a quote from Edward Sapir, who did seminal work in linguistics early in this century.

"Human beings..are very much at the mercy of the particular language which has become the medium of expression for their society...The fact of the matter is that the "real world" is to a large extent built up on the language habits of the group...We see and hear..as we do because the language habits of our community predispose certain choices of interpretation."

At its most basic level, I take Sapir to mean that we get our concepts of such things as "risk" and "safety" from our community—and most particularly from our childhood home environment. And we continue to use these concepts the way we originally received them, without ever examining them to see if their meaning may have been altered over time.

Defining Risk

Our community and household got their basic ideas of "risk" and "safety" from the Great Depression—a massive episode of deflation in which everyone lost his principal. Loss of principal is, indeed, the result that unifies all Americans' experience of the Depression.

If you were living on Park Avenue in 1929, and your store of value was stocks in a margin account, your experience is the same as a farm family's in Des Moines: at the Depression's end, we'd all lost our principal.

Out of this communal experience, we all unconsciously built up the language habit that equates "risk" with "principal." And this closes the unconscious off to other ways of perceiving risk, just as the Hopi language, whose verbs have no tenses, can't express your and my concept of time. The language shapes the experience, and then closes it off to other interpretations.

If we accept "the language habits of our community" and equate "risk" with "principal," we fall into the myth that there may exist a state which we might describe as "no risk." In other words, if risk is principal, and we own an FDIC-insured CD or a Treasury bond, principal is absolutely guaranteed, and is therefore in a state of "no risk." Principal cannot be lost, and risk is principal, so that which assures principal is the antithesis of "risk." It is, in the habitual language of the group, "safety."

Risk is thus something that is either present or absent, given our unconscious use of language. Another seminal linguist, Benjamin Whorf, observed that factory workers were very careful, particularly with their cigarettes, around metal drums that were full of gasoline. They tended to be very careless, and to toss cigarette butts around thoughtlessly, when the drums were "empty"—that is, when there was no gasoline in them. The workers were, Whorf concluded, placing themselves in mortal danger because of their unconscious, shared interpretation of the word "empty."

The "empty" drums were far more dangerous, because they contained highly explosive vapor. (The explosion of a teacup full of gasoline fumes will, for instance, blow a 30-foot boat completely out of the water, as every power-boater knows.) The overriding issue in this situation wasn't chemistry, though; it was language. Or rather, the powerful ability of language to distort thought.

This is a wonderful analogy for the tragically flawed concept of "no risk"—the lunatic notion that an investment can be "empty" of risk, because it contains no "gasoline"; that is, no ability to cause principal loss.

There is no such thing as "no risk." Just as gasoline evaporates into fumes and becomes even more dangerous, "safety of principal" evaporates into "risk of purchasing power." Money is always at risk; it is constantly exposed to one risk or another. A two-year Treasury Bond, as I pointed out last month, contains no risk of principal (gasoline). But it is bursting at the seams with risk of loss of purchasing power (fumes) since, net of inflation and taxes, its return is negative. It is reducing your purchasing power, and therefore, buying such a bond would be like tossing a cigarette butt into the "empty" gasoline drum.

We will not make investors realize this by trying to teach them chemistry (in this analogy, force-feeding them the Ibbotson chart). Rather, we must get them to re-examine their unconscious habits of language, particularly with respect to "risk" and "safety," by pointing out to them the toxicity of groupthink.

If most people were right, most people would be rich. Since most people are not rich, groupthink is, by its very nature, always wrong. The "unconscious language habits of the group" guarantee investment failure.

Framing The Question Correctly

The tragic fiction at the heart of the no-load myth is, of course, that the investor can figure out the answer himself. This conclusion must be wrong, because the premise—that the investor has the question framed right—is fatally flawed.

A 55-year-old, using the toxic linguistic myth of "risk" and "no risk," is certainly capable of picking out the best-performing, lowest-expense-ratio, no-load government bond fund. And, as he writes out his check, he is striking a match—and throwing it into the "empty" gasoline can of "no risk" government bonds.

Twenty-five years from now, the investor and his wife will be (a) alive and kicking, and (b) destitute. The "fumes" (risk of purchasing power) will have exploded, albeit in slow motion. Please note that their fund will have performed superbly as a store of principal. But since, after inflation and taxes, it will have eroded their purchasing power for a quarter of a century, it will quite literally have killed them. No, that's not entirely fair; language will have killed them. Their answer was OK, as far as it went. But their habits of language caused them to frame the question all wrong.

The no-load myth says that what's most important is how your funds perform. So buy no-load funds because they outperform. This is madness.

At the end of your investing lifetime, it won't matter how your funds performed relative to other funds. What your funds do isn't the critical variable. What matters most is what *you* do. What you do (e.g., adding money when your funds are sagging, not when they're soaring) will probably be a pure function of the quality of the advice you get. And good, caring, personal advice is never free.

The advice we professionals give today has got to start with a re-examination of language. When folks say, "stocks are too risky," we have to ask (with or without the prop of the Expo '74 10-cent postage stamp), "How are you defining risk?"

And when they say, "We can't invest in the Great Companies of America; we've got to keep our money safe," you need to ask them, "SAFE FROM WHAT?"

The Next Best Thing To A Buy Signal From God

This catchy title (which wasn't the one I wrote; the magazine changed it) is (a) interesting but (b) unrelated to the real subject of the column—which is systematic withdrawal plans.

It is deeply ingrained in the American financial psyche that, as one draws closer to retirement, one should start switching out of one's equity investments and into bonds. That's because bonds are "safe" and produce "income."

I believe (with, among others, Sir John Templeton) that this view is completely, and very dangerously, wrong. Instead of investing in debt securities for X% income, I believe you should own stock funds, collect the dividends, and invade the principal (until you don't have to anymore) for the difference between the dividend yield and X%.

*In the example I used, X was 7%. I assumed you couldn't get more than 3% in dividends, and that you had, therefore, to start off banging the principal for the other 4% a year. Even with trendline growth of dividends and principal, a stock fund (or funds) would (a) give you your 7% a year without breaking a sweat, (b) completely eliminate principal invasions in about fifteen years, (c) let you grow your income thereafter from dividends alone, and (d) leave you, 20 years later, with **three and a half times your original investment!***

You gotta believe...

The Next Best Thing To A Buy Signal From God

The overwhelming majority of the roughly 160 speeches I gave last year were talks to members of the financial services industry. My message in virtually all of those talks was the same: There's a portfolio crisis of epic proportions brewing in the United States (and, even more so, in Canada). The problem is that people own way too many bonds and not even remotely enough stocks.

As the year went on, I noticed an interesting shift in my business. Brokerage firms, insurance companies and banks to whom I'd made my basic speech began hiring me to come back and give the talk to their clients and prospects. This year, the pace of my talks to the public has accelerated further. And I'm starting to see a pattern.

When I suggest that folks are still defining risk and safety the way their parents did—purely in terms of principal—I see a lot of heads start nodding in agreement. But, I tell them, you're not going to live anything like your parents' lives. Thirty years ago, a man retired at 65 and was dead by 73; his son retires today at 60, and will live to see 84 (the son's 60-year-old bride will see 88).

Thus, in retirement, the average couple will easily live to see prices double. Furthermore, it's a pretty good bet that at least one of the pair will see prices triple. So the risk—here I hold up my 1974 10-cent stamp and my 1994 29-cent stamp—isn't really principal, it's purchasing power. (If the newspaper reports are correct, before long you'll be holding a 32-cent stamp next to that 10-cent stamp.)

Invest In Rising Income Streams

Then I tell 'em to halt. If they're going to be living in a rising cost

165

world for the rest of their lives, they'd better be thinking about investing in some rising income streams. And the only reliable rising income stream I know of (indeed, one that keeps going up even—and especially—when interest rates go down) is the dividends of The Great Companies in America. (Lots of heads nod, and pretty vigorously, too.)

Phillip Morris's dividend, for instance, is higher in 1994 than the price of the stock (adjusted for splits and stock dividends) was in 1974. Why, just last month, the Walt Disney Company raised its cash dividend by 20%. (Wide-eyed heads nodding a mile a minute.) Dividend growth from America's great companies can be your secret weapon against decades of rising prices in retirement.

Then I open it up for questions. And, no later than the third question, I invariably hear: "But What If We Need Income?"

A variation on this theme is, "When do you sell your equity mutual funds?" My answer, of course, is: "Why do you sell your equity mutual funds?" And then I hear, "Because you retire and you need the income."

The automatic assumption is that stocks and income are somehow mutually exclusive—even when people have just listened to my passionate exposition of the magic of dividend growth. "Income," to the great American saver/investor, means "bonds." Moreover, stocks are "high risk" and bonds are "low risk."

The Two-Fold Beauty Of Tough Sales

I beg to differ, and therein lies one of the great sales opportunities of the hour. You see, whenever we can find a huge consensus built up around any popularly held belief (in this case, "income means bonds"), we know two things. (1) The consensus is wrong. (2) If we can make people see that, we can get 'em to move an awful lot of money out of what they want and into what they need.

I don't argue that this is an easy sale; the great ones never are. Show me an asset class that's an easy sale—gold in '81, oil in '82, real estate in '85, stocks in early '87, bonds six months ago—and I'll show you an asset class with at least one, and quite possibly both, front wheels over the cliff already.

But the two-fold beauty of tough sales is that you absolutely know you're right (because most folks don't want to hear you), and you've got no competition (because most salespeople/planners are taking the path of least resistance and giving people what they want, rather than what they need).

It is in this spirit that I commend to your attention that most wonderous (and deeply counterintuitive) of all retirement income vehicles: the systematic withdrawal plan from equity managed accounts (mutual funds, annuities, wrap accounts—I care not: the principle is the same).

You've got to know instinctively that systematic withdrawal plans are great: (a) almost nobody uses 'em; (b) hell, almost nobody's even heard of 'em; (c) when you explain 'em to people, at first they look at you as if you have two heads. These three attributes, taken together, are always the next best thing to a buy signal from God.

Moreover, I think that few, if any, financial planning ideas are likely to produce as many million-dollar tickets over the next 12 months as systematic withdrawal plans. And if you're looking for a seminar topic that is virtually guaranteed to blow the audience's socks off without having to argue or predict the direction of the markets, the systematic withdrawal plan is a major winner. And you can tell the whole story, taking people through a 20-year illustration, in 30 minutes flat, leaving lots of time to take your audience's questions.

Making The Presentation

Like all presentations that rest on one hypothesis, you can't let your argument hide behind a table of numbers. You have to stand up for the hypothesis—in this case, that the long-term return of common stocks is about 11%, which breaks down into 3% dividends and about 8% price appreciation. That's all.

These days, when the market is coming off a decade of returns that are closer to 18% to 19%, this is a very easy thesis to defend. While pointing out the last decade's returns to your prospect/audience, you'll want to appear (and get a lot of silent points for appearing) much more conservative by using the 70-year record. Here's the illustration.

We'll assume that the client has a total investable net worth of $1 million, and needs $70,000 in income from his portfolio. (Just to keep the comparison apples-to-apples, we'll ignore taxes.)

Now, assume that the client puts the whole amount into 7% bonds with a 20-year maturity. You'd have to take more than a bit of credit risk to do that, but never mind. The portfolio produces the needed $70,000 for the whole 20 years, and then the bonds mature, returning the investor's million bucks. Of course, at today's inflation rate, the million bucks has lost about two-thirds of its purchasing power during the 20 years...but never mind, the bonds have accomplished the mission...and no more.

Now, suppose that the million is invested in stocks at a going-in yield of a paltry 3%, which the investor withdraws, for income of $30,000. He gets the other $40,000 he needs by invading principal—here's the counterintuitive part—at the end of the year. Remember, since he's spending the dividends, his remaining appreciation (both in dividends and prices) is assumed to be 8%.

Since his dividend income is going up every year (dividend growth—yes!), the extent to which he has to invade principal to make up his income needs is steadily declining. In fact, in year 16, his dividend income has grown to the full $70,000 of his income needs—and then some.

Because his purchasing power has declined so much by then, let's allow him to continue to pull out his 3% dividend income even after it exceeds $70,000. Indeed, by the 20th year, that 3% will be worth $97,000 to the investor—almost 40% more than the static $70,000 his bonds would have produced.

The incremental income, however, isn't the most dramatic difference between the stock and bond portfolios, is it? No, it's the ending value of the investment that's the real heart-stopping surprise. The bond portfolio matures at the same $1 million, but the stock portfolio—even after 15 years of principal invasion—is worth three and a half times his original investment!

Indeed, how could it not have accreted significantly if you're never pulling more than 7% (and end up only pulling 3%) out of an asset class which, left to its own devices, compounds at around 11%? This just points out again the fact that the critical, core belief here isn't in the arithmetic—it's in the 11%. The core belief, in other words, always has to be in The Great Companies in America. Once you start nibbling around the edges of that belief, the arithmetic is pure poetry.

At that point, you can start looking at alternative scenarios. Remember that the principal-obsessed American saver/investor doesn't look up the dividends in the paper every day: he looks up the prices. This, in turn, is what gives rise to the myth of volatility as risk, a truly lunatic notion. I always tell people that they can prevent stocks prices from seeming volatile if they'll simply stop looking at them. In 1987, if you never looked at prices, but only at dividends, you'd never have known anything was wrong, would you? Know why that was? Because nothing **was** wrong, in any meaningful long-term sense.

Still, you do know (and so do the folks) that stocks just don't march forward at a lock-step 11%. So you'll want to have one or both of two more arrows in your quiver.

One is another theoretical run-out showing what happens to the

The Gronsky Generic Fund—Systematic Withdrawal Plan

Assumptions: $1,000,000 investment, minimum $70,000 income needed. Going-in-dividend-yield 3%. Dividends and prices grow 8% per year. Principal invasions made at year-end. *

Year	3% Dividend Income	Year-End Account Value	Principal Invasion	Net Value of Fund
1	$30,000	$1,080,000	$40,000	$1,040,000
2	31,200	1,123,200	38,800	1,084,400
3	32,500	1,172,000	37,500	1,133,700
4	34,000	1,224,400	36,000	1,188,400
5	35,700	1,283,500	34,300	1,249,100
6	37,500	1,349,000	32,500	1,316,500
7	39,500	1,421,800	30,500	1,391,300
8	41,700	1,502,600	28,300	1,474,400
9	44,200	1,592,300	25,800	1,566,600
10	47,000	1,691,900	23,000	1,668,900
11	50,100	1,802,400	19,900	1,782,500
12	53,500	1,925,100	16,500	1,908,500
13	57,300	2,061,200	12,700	2,048,500
14	61,500	2,212,300	8,500	2,203,800
15	66,100	2,380,100	3,900	2,376,200
16	71,300	2,556,300	-	2,566,300
17	77,000	2,771,600	-	2,771,600
18	83,100	2,993,300	-	2,993,300
19	89,800	3,232,800	-	3,232,800
20	97,000	3,491,400	-	3,491,400

Some intra-year rounding used.

investor if his stock account declines 25% the day after he buys it, and then goes back to its 11%-a-year clip. I'll let you do the arithmetic year-by-year for yourself, but suffice it to say that you end up with $1,850,000 or so even after pulling out your needed $70,000 a year.

The other, even better, item of backup is a real-life illustration from a fund or funds that you like over the last 20 years, or just about any 20-year period you care to name. (But remember, there are very few 20-year periods over which you could have gotten 7% from bonds without invading principal. And, unlike stocks, principal invasion in bonds (a) is gone forever, and (b) starts the portfolio on a downward spiral. Indeed, once you start invading principal in a bond account, you have, in effect, annuitized your capital, and you have to start hoping you die before you run out of money.)

Once you start working on systematic withdrawal plans, you'll think of (and be asked for) a lot of other permutations. And that's fine; that's probably what God was thinking of when She almost simultaneously invented wholesalers and computers. Show the folks their version of reality as well as yours, and you much more than double your chances of getting the order.

And why? In the end, it's because folks simply do not realize how wonderful stocks are, and how they are the almost universal answer to virtually all financial needs—not just for "growth" but especially for "income."

Retaining Client Assets Through Multigenerational Marketing

Over the next twenty years or so, the baby boomers' parents are going to journey to the happy hunting ground—and leave their offspring over $10,000,000,000,000. (Yup: that's ten **trillion** *smackers.) People need help—and, even better, know they need help—arranging for the transfer of this wealth in an efficient way that minimizes taxes. That's where you come in— because, the last time I looked, there was still no such thing as no-load estate planning.*

This article formulated Murray's law of multigenerational marketing, to wit:

"THE PERCENTAGE OF A FAMILY'S ASSETS YOU CONTROL, AND THE LENGTH OF TIME YOU CONTROL THOSE ASSETS, ARE A DIRECT FUNCTION OF HOW MANY FAMILY MEMBERS YOU TALK TO ON A REGULAR BASIS."

My whole point is that if you're the person who's helping a family construct the pipeline through which its assets are flowing intergenerationally, you're going to control those assets—quite literally, for generations.

Insurance companies ordered about a gabillion reprints of this article, which I take to be anecdotal evidence that I was on the right track. See if you agree...

Retaining Client Assets Through Multigenerational Marketing

If you're planning to be in this business a long time, and don't think having to re-build your book every few years is a good use of your time, I'd like to introduce you to a concept I call multigenerational marketing.

Simply stated, the law of multigenerational marketing is as follows: The percentage of a family's assets you control, and the length of time you control those assets, are a direct function of how many family members you talk to on a regular basis.

The classic example is an account where your contact is a successful 55- to 60-year-old businessman. You get along great; you talk every day; you know each other so well that you can just about finish each other's sentences. The wife? In the background somewhere, and besides, as the client makes clear, he makes the financial decisions.

Everything goes along great until one afternoon when the guy gets into an argument with an oncoming crosstown bus about who has the right of way. Your guy loses. And you no sooner see the obituary than you see the transfer papers.

The widow, it turns out, cordially despises you—and you've never spoken to her for five minutes at a stretch. Why the antipathy? Partially because the deceased liked you so much—and the widow holds you indirectly responsible for keeping her in the dark about money.

Opening A Channel Of Communication

This scenario is played out every day. But you can easily avoid it if you make sure you've opened a channel of communication to all the prospective widows in your account book—even if it's just taking both husband and wife to dinner once in a while. And even if finances aren't directly discussed. Just by letting them both know that you're ready to be as helpful to her as they'll let you be, you may insure that crosstown bus doesn't get you, too.

And clearly, stepping up your contact with potential widows— which, actuarially speaking, all married women are—isn't just defensive marketing. Particularly for women in our business, it can be a great, proactive prospecting device.

I've been recommending that firms start doing "widow training seminars," although I'm still struggling to come up with something less blood-curdling to call them. (And maybe I should stop struggling; maybe the best thing to do is just call them what they are.)

You can get a whole host of pertinent agenda items for such a seminar from Alexandra Armstrong and Mary Donahue's wonderful book *On Your Own: A Widow's Passage to Emotional and Financial Well-Being* (published last year by Dearborn Financial Publishing). It would be hard for me to do justice to this terrific book in this brief space; suffice it to say that, whether you're planning seminars or not, everyone in our business should be reading—and giving clients many copies of—*On Your Own.*

The Windfall Wave

Much has been made, in recent years, of the so-called age wave. In our business, we've taken the age-wave phenomenon simply to mean the huge shunt of the nation's 77 million "baby boomers" from their peak spending years to their peak saving years. We've been told (and re-told) to get ready for the crush of these pre-retirees out of their BMW phase and into their mutual fund frenzy phase.

This is all well and good—and it's right up in your face, so you can't miss it anyway. But the spending/saving shunt is only part of the story. The other, and potentially more important, point is that the baby boomers are also going to become the greatest legatees ever in history. And if you are not helping both generations plan that process, chances are you're going to get lost in the shuffle when the actual transfer takes place.

A recent Cornell University study states that baby boomers will inherit $10.4 trillion—nearly twice the current U.S. GNP, and more than half the current sum of all household financial assets, including cash and checking account deposits.

These bequests are estimated to start out at around $85 billion in 1995 (in a million and a half separate transfers) and to peak out in the year 2015, with $335 billion in three and a half million transfers.

If you're proudly and busily helping some graying yuppie with his $1,000-a-month dollar-cost-averaging program, and haven't heard a peep about the half million bucks his father's got earmarked for your guy in a bank trust department, you just bought a one-way ticket to Palookaville. By the same token, if you're Dad's and Mom's advisor, but the kids have never heard of you and could care less, you may just end up being the pallbearer nobody recognized. You've just got to make the generational jump—in whichever direction is necessary—if you're going to be more than a one-generation way station for this family's wealth.

The Grandchild Indicator

One of the easiest ways to open lines of communication to all parts of a family is via the fact that anybody can give anybody $10,000 a year without paying gift tax. So this is a great way to move significant amounts of money intergenerationally without waiting for the estate tax bite.

If you see a little child's photo in your client's home or office, you know you're looking not just at somebody's child, but also a number of people's grandchild or niece/nephew. So, even if this child is the offspring of your relatively penniless 35-year-old client, she's also the grandchild of up to four people, and could, therefore, be accumulating up to $40,000 a year through you—if you'd just ask your client for the introductions.

This is multigenerational marketing at its simplest but most effective. And, of course, the grandchild is never going to be safe from getting a birthday card from you, is she? Because, after all, at $40,000 a year, she could be a millionaire long before she goes to college.

As the pendulum swings back from the transaction-oriented '80s and early '90s to the intensely relationship-oriented future, we all have to find a way to become what our profession used to be about: literally, the family financial advisor. To do that, you can't rest on your laurels when you get a new account. Instead, you have to keep asking yourself and your clients: How many people in this family don't I know yet?

Hallelujah!
A Lousy Market!

*This is the single most widely-reprinted
column yet. And it contains the one idea, out of
all these columns, that people most often repeat
back to me as having helped them change the
way they think of the business:*

*"(IN MARKETS LIKE THIS,) THE AMATEUR
OBSESSES ABOUT HOW UPSET HIS
CLIENTS ARE, AND HE FREEZES UP.
THE PROFESSIONAL FOCUSES ON HOW
UPSET **EVERYBODY ELSE'S CLIENTS
ARE**, AND GOES AFTER THEM LIKE
THERE'S NO TOMORROW."*

*"A bear market," I wrote, "is always played on
the professional's home field, with the attendant
advantage." So many people had come into the
business in the four years between the Saddam
bear market and '94's Greenspan silent spring,
that the deer-in-the-headlights phenomenon was
virtually pandemic by May. But "the professional
knows that periods of great investor distress are
precisely the occasions for him to demonstrate
his tremendous added value."*

*A wise, if cynical, elder of Wall Street told me
a quarter of a century ago that "a bear market is
a period during which common stocks are
returned to their rightful owners." In this article, I
tried to make the point that hugely disappointing
markets like '94 are periods when accounts are
returned to their rightful owners...if we put
ourselves in front of the shell-shocked investor,
and offer to lead him to safety.*

Here's how...

Hallelujah!
A Lousy Market!

I'm finally ready to come out of the closet, and admit what readers of this column may have suspected for a long time: I hate bull markets. Everything about a roaring bull market works against the real professional in this business. Here's why.

1. Bull Markets Extinguish Value. As a bull market goes higher and higher, the real investment pro finds fewer and fewer things he can warmly recommend to his clients with a clear conscience. By its nature, a bull market raises prices to, and then beyond, what investments are really worth. At that point, continuing to recommend things just because they're going up becomes a painful exercise in the greater fool theory.

2. Bull Markets Trivialize The Caution Born Of Long Experience And Reward Recklessness Born Of Inexperience. Professor John Kenneth Galbraith wisely observed, "Financial genius is a short memory in a rising market." As performance mania spreads, investors chase the highest returns, ignoring the professional's warning that this involves taking the highest risks. Why should the investor buy from you something that's been clicking along at 18% a year for the last ten years, when a 23-year-old is calling him with something that's up 80% in the last 12 months? Thus, a bull market encourages the investor to scorn the professional's hard-won instincts, and to buy into the amateur's latest tree that will grow all the way to the sky.

3. Finally, A Bull Market Convinces The Investor That He Can Do It Himself. It therefore maximizes the attraction of "no-load" investments, and sets at naught the investor's perception of the value of your professional services. Performance mania (or, more properly, the toxic illusion that performance is a one-variable equation, irrespective of risk) directs investors toward any no-load fund that's momentarily doing better than the sound investments he paid you to buy. Bull markets encourage in the investor an infantile over-estimation of his own genius and power.

Why I Love Markets That Are Getting Killed

Give me a few more minutes and a couple of more columns of space on the next page, and I'll think of three more reasons why bull markets are so meretricious. But these three are more than sufficient to make the point. So, let's turn now to the real point of this article, which is how much—and why—I love markets that are getting killed.

1. Down Markets Beget Bargains. The amateur is an aggressive buyer when markets are expensive; the professional gets aggressive when prices are in free-fall. The time to buy stocks, as Sir John Templeton has always said, is when "others are urgently and anxiously selling them." Whenever the prevailing emotional current goes from greed to fear, the professional comes into his element. When mutual funds are in net liquidation and there's a bear on *Newsweek's* cover, there's a song in the pro's heart. Is it hard to get people to buy? Sure, but to the professional, that's yet another validation of his bullishness.

The professional knows that value is born out of chaos, and the greatest values—the true lifestyle changers, the turning points in an investment sales career—are born out of the greatest chaos. "I buy," said one of the founders of the Rothschild fortune, "when blood is running in the streets of Paris." (Has anybody noticed the blood running in the streets of Phillip Morris?)

But what if they go lower, you may ask? Then you buy some more, and pound the table even more joyously with prospects who said no on the last go-round. The amateur agonizes over identifying the bottom, and always misses it. (The shortest time period measurable by man is the time between when it's "too soon" to buy stocks and when it's "too late.") The professional is happy to be operating in a zone of great value, and to let nature take its course. In short, the amateur's bear market is the professional's big sale.

2. Bear Markets Paralyze The Amateur And Energize The Professional. A bear market is always played on the professional's home field, with the attendant advantage. The amateur has never seen big downticks before, and does his deer-in-the-headlights act. He stops calling his clients, which embitters them; needless to say, he's long since stopped prospecting.

The professional knows that periods of great investor distress are precisely the occasions for him to demonstrate his tremendous added value. Experience, calm, encouragement, opportunism, steadiness—those are the values the professional brings to the table in a bear market. And they're exactly the qualities of which the investor suddenly feels most in need.

Put another way, the amateur obsesses about how upset his clients are, and he freezes up. The professional obsesses about how upset *everybody else's clients are.* And he goes after them with renewed vigor. Suddenly he's writing a letter to everybody in his prospect card box—a letter full of warmth, encouragement...and the scent of bargains! (And, of course, he's following each and every letter up with a phone call, because just sending out letters is non-prospecting.)

The professional is also giving as many seminars as he can, as fast as he can. And he's packing them in, with the topic: "Your Investments: What You Should Do **Now**." Because the value-added professional knows that the newly chastened investor just wants someone to tell him what to do now.

Just find the energy to tell a whole lot of new people what you believe in times like this. Prospecting is, after all, the ultimate numbers game, and your chances of winning that game are greatest when you have the fewest competitors. That only happens in lousy markets. And the lousier the markets get, the more this wonderful outcome happens.

3. The Accounts You Pick Up In Times Of Adversity Will Be With You For A Very Long Time, And Will Be Great Referral Sources. Friendships formed in combat often last a lifetime. And the bonds you form with a new account during periods of great adversity ("Hang on, buddy; we'll get through this together") are often the real emotional ties that make for career-long relationships. (Whereas the bonds that are formed in bull markets are usually based on "performance," and are, therefore, no bonds at all.)

Moreover, since you'll have repositioned the account in times of low prices, your recommendations will probably look very good before too long, and that really gets the referral machine rolling. The client's mindset is, "This is the person who was not only there for me in my hour of darkness, but who got me to buy stuff that subsequently soared." You'll find that he has a hard time keeping this to himself.

One Step At A Time

The hardest thing to do, of course, is to get people moving at all. I recommend the baby step method—which is, in reality, just dollar-cost averaging coated in warm oil.

Let's say I believe (because, in fact, I do) that this is a particularly good time to start acquiring big-cap growth funds. The truly great growth companies have, as a class, been in the doghouse for well over a year (some of them even longer than that, e.g. pharmaceuticals). Consumer growth started tail-spinning toward the deck when Phillip Morris cut the price of Marlboros, giving rise to the lunatic notion Brands Are Dead. Disney had EuroDisney; the magic is gone. Etc., etc. In other words, these stocks were getting trashed long before it was fashionable for stocks to get trashed.

The amateur says Brands Are Dead. The professional remembers how (or remembers, at least, reading about how) the Nifty Fifty got massacred in '73-'74, and how they rose from the ashes to produce unimaginable wealth for the perspicacious few. He notes that Disney raised its cash dividend 20% a couple of months ago, so maybe the end of the world has been postponed. And his clients, in retirement, are going to be living on their dividends, not on their stock prices.

The baby-step colloquy goes something like this:

You: *Big risk: not losing your money, but outliving it. Your costs of living will go up for decades in retirement, so you need a rising income stream. That means the dividends of the Great Growth Companies in America: Coke, Disney, Wal-Mart, Pepsi, Merck, Toys R' Us, etc. Buy Gronsky Growth Fund.*

Prospect: Too soon. (Note: Not "world coming to an end." Just "too soon.")

You: *Think they'll go down for another year?*

Prospect: No. (Or, if he says yes, you ask if he thinks they'll go down for another two years. Keep expanding the time horizon until he says no, they won't keep going down that long. We'll role-play it out as if he says "No" to one year.)

You: *So they'll turn within the next 12 months?*

Prospect: Yes, but you don't know when.

You: *No, but I know how you can be buying them when it happens. Got one more minute to learn how?*

Prospect: You bet.

You: *Okay. Suppose you knew this fund was going to turn on a dime and start going up tomorrow. How much would you invest?*

Prospect: $25,000.

You: *All right. We don't know it'll turn tomorrow, but we feel very confident it'll turn in the next 12 months, right?*

Prospect: Yes. What are you getting at?

You: *Put $2,000 a month into Gronsky Growth for the next 12 months. You'll be insulated from missing the bottom—indeed, if we're both right, you'll be buying right at the bottom. Oh, and by the way, if we're both wrong, and they've already bottomed, we'll at least be buying some on the way up. Never try to catch the bottom; you can't do it. You just want to be putting serious money in systematically when you're in a ZONE OF GREAT VALUE. Right?*

Prospect: Right.

To all arguments about current events ("Oh yeah? Well what about Whitewater/Serbia/Mexico/Hillary/Smoking Ban/Greenspan?"), I always answer, "Yes, and how about Watergate and the Oil Embargo." After a long silence, the guy says, "Huh?" And I say, "This constitutional crisis, on top of this economic crisis, will surely do us in, right? Can't even think of investing in the Great Companies now. Besides, it's 1974, and everybody knows Growth Is Dead. Hey, nice bell-bottoms." Sooner or later, the guy gets it. The question is: do you?

How To Deal With '94's Cub Market

*Following up "Hallelujah!" I used this column to propose two basic ideas. First was the concept that a market characterized by falling prices (glass half empty) is also a market in which you get terrific rallies in both **value** and **yields** (glass half full...and rising!).*

When he can give his clients better values and higher yields, the professional is energized. When he can no longer hide behind past performance and the illusion of trees that grow all the way to the sky, the amateur curls up under his desk in the fetal position, and begins to moan.

*The second theme this column develops is my belief that Americans aren't risk-averse, they're **loss**-averse—and they can't distinguish between fluctuation and loss.*

*Because by the time this article appeared, **government bond funds were in net redemption!** Here you had the highest quality debt instruments ever crafted by the hand of man...making timely payment of principal and interest per Uncle Sam's ironclad guarantee...and people were jumping out of windows because N.A.V. was doing the Greenspan swan dive! ("I thought you told me this was guaranteed!" wailed America, and reached for the phone to call its attorney, Bernie.)*

I argued, in this piece, that you could become rich and famous and live forever...if you could just remind people that fluctuation isn't loss. It's just...fluctuation.

Don't call 'em bear markets, I counseled; call 'em Big Sales.

High prices: bad. Low prices: good...

June, 1994

How To Deal With '94's Cub Market

I've been amazed at the depth of people's reaction to the recent unpleasantness in the markets—both investors' reactions and ours. My concerns crystallized when a very highly placed industry marketing executive, in a conversation we were having about the drop-off in his company's sales, called this a bear market.

Excuse me, but a 10% overall decline isn't a bear market. It's a *cub* market. Or rather, it's a crosstown-bus market: ordinarily, if you miss the last 10% decline, you just stand there for 15 minutes, and another comes along.

I take for granted that even a cub market spooks the investor. My concern is the effect it's having on us. Let me offer another example.

Not long ago, I gave an all-day sales workshop for a group of investment reps. When I opened the floor for discussion topics, the first question was, "How do you do business in a market like this?"

I let the question hang in the air for a moment, and then I asked, "Does everybody understand this question?" Unanimous nods. "Does everybody agree that this is an important topic right now?" Unanimous, and very vigorous, nods. "Very well," I said. "I'll be happy to discuss it with you, if someone will just tell me what it means."

There followed several moments of strangled silence; you could just feel the conviction spreading through the room that the old guy had clearly lost his marbles.

When I couldn't bear it anymore, I said, "Let me understand you. The Great Sales Manager in the sky has just marked down the prices of everything you sell by 10% to 30%. These are the first markdowns of this magnitude we've had since 1990 for stocks, and since 1987 for bonds. In other words, we've having terrific rallies in both *values* and *yields*!

"And you're asking me how you do business in a market like this? I've got a better question. How the hell did you do business six months ago?"

The group was an excellent one, and quickly (albeit ruefully) took my none-too-subtle point. I was asking, quite literally, who said "this market" was either bad or hard to do business in? Clearly, it couldn't be anybody who's a real professional in this business. (For a refresher course in the ways in which amateurs and professionals distinguish themselves from each other in markets "like this," see *Hallelujah! A Lousy Market!* in last month's issue.)

So, if professionals didn't say it, maybe the culprit was an amateur in this business, yes? No, that theory doesn't hold water, either. Amateurs don't have their own ideas; amateurs don't act, they react—to someone else's ideas.

And who are they reacting to? Why, to the investing public, of course. And not just one or two isolated investors, but the consensus of investors...which is, unfortunately, always wrong.

You see, if most folks were right, most folks would be rich. Most folks are manifestly not rich, thanks in large part to the fact that they love markets like the fourth quarter of '93 and they don't love markets "like this."

In other words, the consensus is wildly counterintuitive. It loves investments when their prices have been marked up to historically high levels, and then hates those investments when they're "on sale." They'd never react to the price of canned tuna in the supermarket the way they do to the Dow Jones Industrial Average.

If the price of tuna doubled over a four-year period, you'd expect consumption to plummet, as people looked elsewhere for their protein. But, come a sudden 10% to 30% markdown, buyers would flock back in...wouldn't they?

Sure they would. Because, in every aspect of our economic life, our unconscious mantra is—High prices: bad. Low prices: good.

But when people walk through the magic door marked investments, something profoundly weird happens. Suddenly (though still unconsciously), it's high prices: good. Low prices: bad. And the question we professionals have to ask ourselves is: are we, without realizing it, buying into this deeply counterintuitive malaise?

The Nature Of The Beast

The problem, I believe, is that we continue to assume that we're dealing with something called risk-averse investors. But all of my experience suggests that Americans are neither risk-averse nor investors. Instead, they are *loss-averse savers.*

Loss-averse is different from risk-averse. Americans are conscious of only one financial danger: the loss of their principal. This is a risk, I grant you. A fairly low-level risk, and one that's very easy to defend against: all you need to wipe it out are diversification and time.

Americans don't see that, do they? They're fatally obsessed with the neurotic need for the number of units of the currency they have always to be constant. They don't need it to go up, as long as it doesn't go down. In other words, Americans are afflicted with the deeply ahistorical notion that the *currency, in and of itself, is a long-term store of value.*

It isn't, of course, but that's not the point. Why do people think it is?

The answer is the so-called Great Depression, an event in which the currency (together with things like government bonds, which are essentially proxies for the currency) was the only thing that held its value. The business, the bank, the stocks, the farm...even the house: all lost their value.

Which brings me to my other point: that Americans aren't investors at all; they're savers. An investor, I believe, is someone who looks forward, into the future, with faith. A saver, on the other hand, looks back, into the past...with fear. Somewhere back there, his mother and father assured him, is a financial holocaust which, because it happened before, can and will happen again...without warning. Only if the number of units of the currency you have is "guaranteed" at all times are you "safe."

Time out for a reality check. The event universally called The Great Depression was, in reality, The Great Deflation. We've only had three years in the 20th Century in which the Consumer Price

Index declined by more than 1%—and they were three years in a row: '30, '31 and '32. Hasn't happened before or since. It's the ultimate financial anomaly. (And deflation is, of course, the only economic scenario in which the currency gains value.)

Yet the great American loss-averse saver awaits the second coming with never-ending fear. And soon, he'll go to the Post Office to pay 32 cents for a first-class stamp that cost 6 cents in 1971, little more than two decades earlier. And he still won't understand what risk truly is...

Fluctuation Isn't Loss

What we need to say to the loss-averse saver is simply: There are, in the end, only two things you can do with your capital. You can save it, or you can invest it.

The great thing about savings (bank accounts, CDs, Treasury bills, money market funds) is that your principal stays virtually constant all the time. There's tremendous emotional comfort in knowing that the number of dollars you had yesterday is the same number you have today, and that it'll be the same number tomorrow.

And you pay a truly terrible price for that emotional comfort. (In fact, if you live long enough, you pay a fatal price.) It is simply that savings virtually always produce a negative return, after you account for inflation and taxes. In other words, your savings are always losing value, but you see that only when you understand what value really is. And what it isn't.

Value isn't implicit in the number of units of currency you have. It's implicit in what that currency will buy. If the prices of everything you need are constantly rising (if, as you will, you pay 32 cents next year for a stamp that cost six cents in '71), that's another way of saying your paper dollars are declining in value. The currency is not, in and of itself, a store of value.

To truly store value—to obtain a return that's positive after inflation and taxes—you need investments...as distinguished from savings. And the great thing about investments—for example, shares in America's great companies—is that, over time, they keep you ahead of inflation and taxes. And you pay a price for that, too. The price is that the dollar value of investments fluctuates...up, mostly, but down once in a while...like now.

The most important thing to remember is that fluctuation isn't loss...unless you choose to make it so, with a panicky sell decision.

Sixty-two years ago, the Dow Jones Industrial Average touched 40—if only for one day. This past January, it touched 4000—if only for one day *so far*. What's been the great risk of that period? I'd say it was not owning 'em. And when was the right time to buy them? Yes: whenever you had the money.

Never mistake savings for investments. And, above all, never mistake your paper dollars for a long-term store of value, because they just aren't. When you get a bigger phone bill this July than you got last July for exactly the same number of phone calls...you've got to know that your dollars have lost some value. But the phone company's shareholders got higher dividends, didn't they? And chances are that, albeit with plenty of temporary fluctuations in between, they've seen the value of their shares rise, as well. And they deserve to...after all, they're investors.

Stop Saying Volatility

Please note the very careful—and very, very soothing—choices of words in the foregoing. I didn't say "stocks," or "the stock market." I said "America's great companies." I didn't say "the price of their stock went up." I said "they've seen the value of their shares rise." I used very down-home illustrations—stamps, your phone bill—things people really relate to (as opposed to, just for example, the Ibbotson chart).

And, above all, I said "fluctuation," not "volatility." Never, never say the word "volatility." It is a code word, invented in October '87 by your enemy, journalism, to hurt you.

In journalismspeak, "volatility" means only one thing: down a lot in a hurry. Sharp, sudden upward price movements are never described as "volatile." Thus, the market's last mad dash from Dow 3600 to 4000 was not "volatile," but the retreat back to 3600 was! (The same is true—only more so—of the seven-week, 700-point spike in the Dow after Desert Storm. The word "volatility" never once passed journalists' snarling lips.)

The concept "volatility-as-risk" is deeply attractive to the principal-obsessed American loss-averse saver. ("If it *can* go down a lot in a hurry, then it *will* go down a lot in a hurry. And it will never come back...just like Mom always said!") You only make it worse by saying the word. So don't. Instead, you can change the whole emotional experience by referring to "perfectly normal fluctuations...the kind you accept in exchange for staying ahead of taxes and inflation."

When you're in a plane, the emotional experience of clear air turbulence is markedly different when the captain chuckles that he's "gonna have to turn on that pesky seat belt sign" than it would be if he came on the P.A. and commenced to scream. Your saying the word "volatility" is, I'm convinced, the moral equivalent of a pilot screaming.

Keep Repeating Your Mantra

Somewhere along in here, it might also be salutary to remember that most everything "bad" that's happened in recent months attends upon the Fed's response to how strong the economy is! This ain't bank holidays and breadlines, folks; this is everything suddenly going too good, too fast.

Our economy is shooting the lights out (as I have been saying it would, in this column, for three years). This is downright spooky, when you think about it, because we're the largest exporter in the world, and our biggest trading partners are only just starting to get up off the canvas. What's going to happen when Europe and Japan really get rolling? Lots and lots more good things, is my guess.

So even if this cub market grows up to be a real bear (as I hope it will), let's welcome it with open arms. Because it may very well be the last big sale of the 20th century. (And remember, we professionals don't call 'em Bear Markets; we call 'em Big Sales.)

So be of good cheer. Keep prospecting like there's no tomorrow. And keep repeating your mantra, to anyone who'll listen: High prices: bad. Low prices: good.

The Great Value Rally of 1994: A Seminar Program

The tuna fish analogy from June's column seemed to make people feel so much better that, the next month, I expanded it, somewhat tongue-in-cheek, to a seminar program, complete with slides. (And I know this column hit a home run, because my phone immediately went into meltdown from people calling to ask if they could buy the slides!)

All it really says is: you hate it when the things you need to buy are marked way up in price: you love it—and you back up the truck—when they're marked down. Your unconscious mantra is: high prices, bad. Low prices, good.

So how come you feel and behave the opposite way toward investments? How can you hate, loathe and fear equities at Dow 1700 (on October 19, 1987) and love them with a purple passion at 4000 (on January 31, 1994)?

What if, before you ever read the next mutual fund prospectus your investment rep sent you, you went through it with a magic marker? And everywhere it said "mutual fund" (or "convertible bonds," or "emerging markets") you crossed those two words out...and wrote in two other words:

TUNA FISH!

Are you chuckling just a little bit? Good. That's what this column was for.

The Great Value Rally of 1994: A Seminar Program

This is, as I suggested a couple of months ago, a simply wonderful time for the professionals in our business to be doing seminars.

First, the folks are awfully confused and scared, so they're looking for somebody to tell 'em it's going to be all right. Second, the amateur in the business is hiding under his desk, leaving the field relatively clear for the professional.

So this month, I thought it might be useful as well as fun to provide you with a seminar presentation which you can put on with a minimum of fuss, feathers—and specificity. This isn't a product seminar so much as it is an *attitude* seminar.

You see, I think that there are only two possible outcomes to any client seminar. One is that the presenter gets worn down by the audience, and he ends up as sad, bored, enervated and anxiety-ridden as they are. And the other outcome, of course, is that the audience ends up as confident and positive as the presenter was—without necessarily knowing why. (Why ask why, anyway?)

Clearly, we want the second outcome. We want the audience to say, "Gee, that investment professional made me feel a whole lot better about things. Now I need to go see him/her to find out exactly what he/she thinks I ought to do."

So here goes, complete with slides:

SLIDE ONE

The Great Value Rally of 1994

MURRAY PRODUCTIONS

Folks, thanks very much for coming to our seminar tonight. We're excited about the terrific opportunities that the current environment presents—not least of all because most people *aren't* excited. Most folks are scared…which tells you that it's way too late to get scared.

You see, if most folks were right, most folks would be rich. Since most folks sure aren't rich, we at (FIRM) like to try to figure out what most folks are thinking. Then, we enthusiastically recommend that our clients and friends go out and do the opposite.

Our theory is that most folks are very aggressive when it'd really pay to be cautious, and very cautious when it's time to be bargain hunting. Clearly, it's bargain hunting time. We call it THE GREAT VALUE RALLY OF 1994.

You see, in the world of investments, when the *prices* of investments go *down*, the relative *values* of those investments go up. Most folks don't see that. They love it when prices go up—even though that usually means value is going down.

> **SLIDE TWO**
>
> **When Prices Go Down,**
>
> **Values Go Up**
>
> MURRAY PRODUCTIONS

For instance, suppose you know of a stock that's going to earn $5 a share this year. We'd advise you to love that stock at $40, tolerate it at $60, and look for something else to buy at $80. Because as the *price* goes up, the *value* of that same $5 in earnings is being ground down.

Most folks, of course, are hiding in the basement at $40…and taking a second mortgage to buy with both hands at $80. They seem to forget that, in investing as well as every other aspect of their economic life…

> **SLIDE THREE**
>
> **High Prices, Bad.**
>
> **Low Prices, Good.**
>
> MURRAY PRODUCTIONS

(Broker reads the slide, then invites the audience to read it aloud with him:) Yes, high prices, bad. Low prices, good. That's the guiding principle of all economic behavior…*except in investing*. (Note: if the audience hasn't started chuckling by now, you're in trouble. If it hasn't started laughing out loud by the end of the next slide, you're dead.)

You see, most folks would never behave in a supermarket the way they do with their investments.

What are you paying for a small can of tuna fish in the supermarket these days? (Audience agrees on a number; say $1.39.) OK, now suppose you walked in tomorrow, and saw a big sign:

Well, you'd probably squint at it for a moment, figuring that the fella might have just misplaced the decimal point, or something. When you realized the sign was right, you'd have said thanks, but no thanks: (1) that's way more than the usual price range, and (2) there's a half dozen other protein sources in the supermarket that you can substitute for tuna, at a calorie-equivalent price of $1.39, right? In effect, you'd have said, "high prices: bad."

Naturally, everybody had the same reaction, and now the market is stacked to the rafters with unsold cans of tuna. Now the manager has to mark 'em down and move 'em out. So the $4.89 is crossed out, and now it's 79 cents. What do you do? Back up the truck, of course, before the guy changes his mind, and before your neighbors buy all the tuna. What's happened? He's lowered the price...and rallied the value! LOW PRICES: *GOOD!*

Can you see where we're going with this? Sure you can! Everybody was wild to buy stocks when the Dow was at 2400 in August '87. It was a NEW HIGH! Uh-oh; most folks forgot. High prices, *bad!*

Well, quicker than you could say "tuna fish," it was October 19, one of the biggest one-day value rallies of modern times. Indeed, it was probably the biggest one-day sale of the century—20% off the great companies in America—something you see once in an investing lifetime. *And most people hated it!* Seems they forgot: LOW PRICES, GOOD!

Sure enough, the Dow went up about 75% from those lows, and it did so in just less than three years. And folks loved it! Just couldn't get enough. Iraq massing troops on the border of Kuwait? Hey, no problem. Those guys are always squabbling with each other about something.

Well, sure enough, we had an invasion in the Middle East, an oil price shock and the onset of a fairly serious recession all at once. And, once again, tuna...uh, sorry: *equities*...went on sale—20% or so in just one turning of the leaves of summer into fall. And most folks got paralyzed.

You're getting the hang of this—I can just feel it!

Yes, from the Desert Shield lows of October '90 (LOW PRICE: GOOD!), we went up about 60% in the next 40 months, touching Dow 4000 at the tippy-top of January 31, 1994. At that point, most folks were happier than ever. Why, mutual funds have been around since 1924...but over 40% of today's mutual fund assets came in on this last run, pictured on this slide. A 60% markup on the tuna fish...and most folks thought that was good!

And so, of course, it was time for another tuna fish sale. Hasn't been much of a sale, as sales go: just about 10%. So maybe they're going to mark the tuna down some more. (1) We don't know. And (2) that's not the point!

The idea here isn't to try to call market tops and bottoms—something which nobody, and I mean *nobody*, can consistently do. What we're trying to do is get you to see that most folks behave toward the great companies in America in a deeply counterintuitive way. When prices are marked way up, people love it, and can't wait to buy more. When prices are marked down, people are scared to death. Not only don't they want to buy any more tuna fish, but they're seriously thinking of selling what they already have in the pantry.

And so, the moral of this story is: *it's all tuna fish.*

All investments are cyclical. When prices are high, and everybody loves 'em, that's the time to stay home for a while. When prices are low, and headlines are scary, most folks don't want 'em. And that's where, historically, the great opportunities lie.

What are we selling tonight at this seminar? Nothing in particular—except plain common sense, and the courage to zig just a little, when "most folks" around you are zagging. We'll be happy to take questions now.

You can do this seminar anytime, anywhere—call the Kiwanis and Rotary, and see if they wouldn't like a nice, non-threatening, fifteen-minute presentation. And see if the folks don't start migrating back to your level of confidence.

Coping With Prospects' Weird Unconscious Equations

I thought it was time, as the summer drew to a close, to dust off and sharpen many of the "toxic definition" and "rose is not a rose" verbal issues which, I found, were once again paralyzing both reps and clients.

My slant on these issues in this column was that the public treats them as one-variable equations. That is, there's something terribly wrong with (fill in the blank: utilities, government bonds, stocks in general, whatever). And that one critically flawed wrong thing explains why you can't buy 'em today...or maybe ever.

The therapeutic approach I recommended in this piece was not to argue ("The stated objection is always the tar baby"). Instead, ask people to see that, in efficient markets, every economic detriment or cost must have an offsetting benefit somewhere in the equation. (For example, "Stocks can go down and CDs can't" is twinned with "Stocks can go up and CDs can't." "If I own a triple-A bond, I'm guaranteed to get my money back; you can't say that about stocks," is matched with "If you own a triple-A bond, you are guaranteed not to be repaid any **more** than you invested; shares of great businesses can—and historically have— multiplied your investment many times over.")

Balancing benefits and costs calmly, dispassionately and (above all) non-argumentatively is the best therapy for the dreaded Weird Unconscious Equation.

Coping With Prospects' Weird Unconscious Equations

Panicking out of one's investments at the first sign of a double-digit price decline is, after all, as American as apple pie. So this month, I'd like to amplify one comment I made in my June column (*How To Deal With '94's Cub Market*) to the effect that fluctuation isn't loss. It's just...fluctuation.

And fluctuation is the (purely psychological, as opposed to financial) price you pay for achieving positive real returns on your investments—as opposed to negative real returns on your (nonfluctuating) savings.

To deal effectively with these issues, you need to remember, above all else, that Americans don't make their financial decisions in their intellect. They make those decisions in their emotions, and then justify what they've decided with their intellect. Thus the objection "I'm not going to do anything now because of...the plunging value of the dollar, and how it's upset the markets" usually means "I'm very scared; I don't understand anything anymore; I'm just so scared."

Avoid The Tar Baby

If you accept the stated (intellectual) objection—something no reader of the last 70 pages of my book *Serious Money* would ever do—and try to answer that objection...you end up like Br'er Rabbit, punching and kicking the tar baby. *The stated objection is always the tar baby.*

You can intellectualize all you want about how the dollar may be down against the yen and the mark, but the trade-weighted dollar—that is, the dollar versus all of the countries we trade with, weighted for actual trade activity—isn't down much at all. In fact, the dollar versus the currencies of two of our largest trading partners, Canada and Mexico, is actually up. "Well," says the prospect, "I just want to wait and see." Which means nothing more or less than "If I don't buy anything, I can't lose my money, and I'm scared I'll lose my money."

You see, Americans don't perceive that there is a time risk in doing nothing. The fact that, six months from now, the prospect will be six months closer to retirement with nothing to show for it doesn't strike terror in an American's heart. The fear of principal loss overwhelms all other concerns.

Nor, for that matter, does it occur to Americans that there is an economic benefit twinned with every economic detriment. Americans get their economic thinking, God help them, from journalism, which is the leading proponent of the one-variable equation. And that one variable is always bad.

Thus, the same people who were worried about our trade deficit with Japan six months ago are now petrified about the declining dollar versus the yen, apparently not seeing that the latter cures the former.

That is, if the dollar is cheap against the yen, Japan will buy a lot of stuff from us. And if the yen is really costly against the dollar, we won't buy their cars, we'll buy ours. Let that go on for a while, and the trade deficit disappears.

Watch Out For Woo-eee

Even when you read this erudite argument, your eyes start to glaze over, don't they? You're tempted to say, "Spare me the two-bit economics lesson, Nicky; just tell me how to get the guy to move."

That just demonstrates how instinctively you reject all left-brain, analytical solutions to problems you know are emotional. The professional isn't selling at times like this, so much as he/she is doing therapy for paralyzing fear. And a skilled therapist doesn't argue the facts, he questions the feelings.

Americans' fear springs from a disabling emotional disturbance, the technical term for which (I just decided) is Weird Unconscious Equations, or WUE (pronounced "Woo-eee"). All WUEs, as we've seen, are one-variable equations, and the one variable is always bad.

Treating Woo-eee

So the salesperson/planner/therapist just has to watch for the central WUE in the prospect's belief system, and then gently question its one-sidedness. Here are some examples:

• **Risk=Principal Loss**—This is the mother of all WUEs (i.e., the MOAWUE, pronounced "MO-WOO-EE!" The accent moves to the first syllable, and the "A" is silent.) The salesperson/planner/therapist says, soothingly, "Yes, principal loss is a risk, and a serious risk, not to be taken lightly. But (holding up his business card with the 1994 29-cent stamp and the 1974 10-cent stamp) have you considered that there may be other risks in your life—some even more real than the risk of losing principal?

"And let's also ask about the good things that come to you when you accept a little principal loss risk. If I own a CD, I have no principal-loss risk. If I own a portfolio of very high quality utility stocks—AT&T, Duke Power, Montana Power, and five dozen other great names like that—I've taken on some principal loss risk. Not much, but some.

"In a rational world—or in an efficient market, which is another way of saying the same thing—nobody would take on principal loss risk (or any risk) if he didn't have to, unless there was some very significant potential benefit that outweighed that risk.

"In the case of great utility stocks, it's that many or most public utilities are government-regulated monopolies. The state of Montana may not love Montana Power, but it's not going to go out and charter a start-up enterprise, Bob and Ethel's Discount Power Company. If you want light and heat anywhere in the great state of Montana, it's Montana Power, or start rubbing two sticks together real fast. This tends to limit the chance that the company will go out of business.

"Moreover, good utility companies raise the dividend that they pay their shareholders most every year—not least of all because they raise the rates they charge their customers. Did your electric and phone bills go up in the last 12 months? So did somebody's dividend checks. Why them and not you?"

Principal loss is a big, amorphous, anxiety-producing concept. You dispel anxiety with comforting, real-life truths that are clear and specific. Above all, you dispel anxiety by talking about great companies, *not* about stocks...or even bonds. And remember: diversification and time always overcome the risk of principal loss. *Always.* You believe that, don't you? Then let the light of your belief (and not the smoke of all the incomprehensible technical details you know) shine on your prospects.

And speaking of utilities, their power-dive of recent months brings us to a prevailing WUE.

• **Fluctuation=Loss**—It's been so long since people saw any decline in their investments (indeed, anybody who bought a mutual fund after October of 1990 may never have seen one) that this "cub market" really has 'em treed.

Many avid buyers of utility funds in 1993 fell victim to the WUE that states HY=HY+0 (T/O). Which means, of course, Higher Yield equals Higher Yield and no Trade-Offs.

But, once again, there's no one-variable equation. If you buy an incremental economic benefit, you take on an incremental economic cost. In the case of utility stocks, it's their tendency to trade down during a general rise in interest rates. But that's fluctuation. It isn't loss...unless the investor makes it so by panicking.

People who know they're investing in companies realize that fluctuation isn't loss. But people who think they're buying stocks don't realize it. The greatest investor in companies of modern times, Warren Buffett, is also the guy who said that unless you're prepared to see a stock's price decline 50% after you buy it, *don't buy it.*

Buffett's saying, of course, that the long-term values of companies are knowable, but the short-to-intermediate-term action of stock prices is not knowable...and doesn't matter. Fluctuation isn't loss. It's...fluctuation.

One antidote to panic about fluctuation is to stop following prices altogether, and follow dividends, instead. If you didn't get monthly statements, couldn't find a newspaper and had a broken TV, you couldn't follow prices, could you? All you'd have to go on, in order to monitor your investments, would be your dividend checks. (This is just as true for bond funds as for stock funds.)

Well, if your only input was your dividend checks, you wouldn't know anything was wrong, would you? Ever wonder why that is? Because nothing is wrong, that's why. Prices are just...fluctuating. And their ability to fluctuate down every little once in a while is the psychological cost of the immense economic benefit of their ability to fluctuate up, which they do most of the time.

There's nothing technical about this. You don't need an Ibbotson chart, a scattergram, or a computer printout to make this point. It's just plain common sense. And a little faith.

A kissin' cousin to the WUE "Fluctuation Equals Loss" is the dreaded:

- **Volatility=Risk**—I have, on several occasions, banned the use by investment professionals of the word "volatility." (And I hope you didn't mistake this for a request. I mean, I hope you're not going around using the word "volatility" and thinking I won't know. I will know...and I'll be very, very angry.)

But this doesn't stop the investing public from using it. Because they get their vocabulary from journalism, which uses the word "volatility" as part of the unspoken WUE—"Volatility Equals Risk." The one bad variable in this equation is that volatility is always a sharp, sudden downward move in prices. A sharp uptick is never "volatile." (These days, it's a "technical rally from an oversold condition.")

In this WUE, "volatility" is just "fluctuation" on a larger scale. That is, it's the ability of downward movements in price to produce "losses" that are bigger and faster than normal.

But I say again: in a properly diversified portfolio, with a proper long-term perspective, "volatility" isn't "risk" any more than "fluctuation" is "loss." The biggest risk of the securities of America's great companies has always been, and continues to be, not owning them. And "losses" in America's securities markets are always temporary unless the investor makes them permanent by panicking.

So I would like to propose a three-variable equation, one that would probably make a 100% better investor out of at least half of all Americans. My rule is that value and yield are always inversely related to price. Hence: LP=HV & HY. Which means, of course, Lower Prices=Higher Values and Higher Yields. (The converse is also true, which, as I mentioned a couple of months ago, is why I Hate Bull Markets.)

We are, as all Americans are keenly aware, going through one of those increasingly rare periods of LP (Lower Prices). It must follow as night follows the day, then, that we're in a period of HV (Higher Values) and HY (Higher Yields). That's how it works.

Anybody looked at the trailing 12-month P/E of the Dow Jones Industrial Average lately? From a 1992 high of perilously close to 30, it's now in the process of nosing below 20. Not dirt cheap, by any measure, but a hell of a lot cheaper (that is, Higher Value) than it's been in a long time. And what gave rise to these higher values? Lower prices, of course.

So, just keep repeating your mantra, to all who will listen: High Prices, Bad. Low Prices, Good!

And just keep doing therapy on those toxic, one-variable WUEs. Because every temporary market decline allows you to permanently capture higher values and higher yields.

And most of all: go easy on the facts. Concentrate on the Truth.

Undersell Your Way
To Success

The essential message of this column is very straightforward, and doesn't need to be synopsized here. I would, however, point out that the thing people seemed to love in this piece was the concept that
"LONG TERM FINANCIAL SECURITY IS ALWAYS PURCHASED AT THE PRICE OF SHORT-TERM INVESTMENT INSECURITY."

And things that give you short-term security—investments that feel good and safe right here and now—invariably lead to long-term financial insecurity...because, after inflation and taxes, they're grinding your purchasing power into sand.

The other point this piece makes is that the act of underselling (or overselling) rewards (or punishes) itself. When you're underselling, your energy accretes because of your growing self-esteem...so you're able to talk to more people, and do more business. Overselling depletes your energy because it makes you feel dirty and ashamed, so you talk to fewer people...and have to oversell those few even harder. It's the ultimate downward spiral.

I conclude that "underselling is great for the clients...but even better for you."

Undersell Your Way To Success

'Tis the season for a new wave of "high-yielding, low-risk" debt funds to blow up in people's faces. It happens about every three years.

This time around, fund managers were reaching for extra yields with derivatives. Now derivatives are really cool when you use 'em to lock in small spread differentials and/or limit risk. They're bad when they're used to make bets, i.e., if rates just drop a little bit more, Gronsky Government Fund will outperform all the government funds in its class.

This distinction is entirely lost on the press, of course. Since journalism is our leading distiller of one-variable equations, we're now being bombarded with D=EI (which means Derivatives equal Evil Incarnate.)

Another unlooked-for but very real outcome of the derivatives blowup has been the official and very vitriolic end of the press's love affair with mutual funds. In August, both the *New York Times* and *The Wall Street Journal* did exposé-style front-page "stories" about the hidden horrors of funds.

Six or seven years ago, it was "government plus" funds. That was called strike one; the press mostly let it pass. Then, about three years ago, it was short-term global income funds, with their myth of the "perfect hedge." (An oxymoron right up there on a par with "jumbo shrimp" and "water landing.") Strike two. (In fairness to debt funds, strike two-and-a-half was the mini-scandal of fund managers trading for their own accounts, which was basically a stock fund phenomenon.)

Then came the high hard one of derivatives (on top of perfectly normal bond market declines due to interest rates), and that was strike three.

When are we going to learn? Reaching for the highest nominal yield, while continuing to sell the illusion of "safety," is the ultimate one-way ticket to Palookaville. It kills you every single time. Why? Because it's good for transactions and bad for relationships, which is the opposite of what we're all supposed to be trying to do. Overselling always sets you up to fail; underselling always, always sets you up for long-term success.

Transactions Versus Relationships

Overselling is always transaction-oriented, and always sows the seeds of the relationship's destruction. ("Buy this fund *now* because it's going to outperform all similar funds *starting this afternoon!*") Underselling is always relationship-oriented and always focuses on the client's long-term comfort level.

You have to say to your client: "I'm not sure this fund will ever be at the top of *Money* magazine's pick-hits-of-the-week list because the manager, Grey Trueheart, has always told me he won't take the sorts of risks you have to take to be Number One. His attitude is: no one is consistently hot, so if it's a choice—and it is—he'd rather be consistent than hot. Do you see why I think that his style is such a perfect fit with your risk-averse attitudes?"

Thus, underselling works to promote healthy client relationships in two important ways. At the front-end, underselling automatically causes you to de-select prospects who are crazy. Somebody who's looking to his investments to supply the missing excitement in his life is going to be bored being undersold. So he'll go elsewhere and take years off some other rep's life with his psychotic episodes. Someone who heaves a deep sigh of relief when you talk about consistency and risk-aversion is probably going to be a high-gain, low-pain relationship for many years to come.

Where underselling really earns its stripes, however, is in a lousy market. That's when the hollowness of overselling shows up in all its ugly, recriminatory aspects. And it's where the underseller shines. You say: "We always agreed that fluctuation is the inevitable price you pay for superior returns. And, as the old song says, here's that rainy day. They've rallied both the values and the yields of just about everything we own. Is there any chance you could put some more money in at these bargain levels?"

Underselling As Moral Leadership

Selling will always be an intrinsic part of what we do, because being a good investor doesn't come naturally to Americans. (If most folks had good instincts, most folks would be rich. Since most folks clearly ain't rich, getting people to invest well will always be a sales job...no matter how consultative the selling is.)

You can't hypnotize or fool people into becoming good investors. You have to ask them to become, in some very real sense, better than they are. Underselling makes good investors, just as surely as overselling makes bad investors. And that's why I see underselling as an act of genuine moral leadership.

When the prospect says, "Why can't I take some more time to think about it?" the overseller says, in effect, "Because it might go to the moon any minute now!" The underseller says, "Because there may be—and there usually is—a terrible price to be paid for doing nothing. When you defer investing in great long-term vehicles because of essentially short-term worries, you may miss the fact that your goals—college, retirement—are extremely date-specific.

"The bursar of Whatsamatta U won't put off your son's first tuition payment for six months because you decided to just watch the markets for six months. Nor will your employer defer your retirement date.

"And the sad thing is: the picture doesn't usually become crystal clear until it's too late. So you only have history to fall back on—and history really teaches us faith in the future, not fear of it.

"Why, every day from 1932 until 1994, when the Dow Jones Industrial Average was going from 40 to 4000, there was always some problem that appeared insurmountable—sometimes lots of problems. Those problems are gone now, and the people who invested in spite of them are financially secure.

"That's the way it works in America: long-term financial security is always purchased at the price of short-term investment insecurity.

"And sadly, the converse is also true: short-term security feels nice, but always leads to long-term insecurity. You have money in

CDs, money market funds...you've got what I call short-term security. But those kinds of instruments, after you account for inflation and taxes, are pulling down your net worth—not building it up.

"At some point, you turn around and find that your net worth is wholly inadequate to your long-term needs. Hence: short-term security has somehow become long-term insecurity. I don't want to see that happen to you; you don't deserve it."

Good People Just Want The Truth

What kind of person can resist that approach? Probably the kind of person with whom you could never build a trusting long-term relationship, anyhow. Let 'em go.

Good people just want to hear the truth, and they're smart enough to know that sometimes the truth hurts. The truth is that if people think and reason and invest the way everybody else does, they get about the same results everybody else gets...which are pretty lousy.

If you're primarily focused on your month, you'll miss this beautiful truth...and stretch to make a transaction happen. Don't. Stay focused on your career. After all, you can't ask people to concentrate on the long term in their investments if you're not willing to do the same thing with your business.

Does that mean you have to prospect more people in order to find the real quality accounts? Of course it does. (You're a good person, so I just knew you'd want to hear the truth.)

Because, in the end, all issues of overselling and underselling are decided by the number of people you're talking to.

The more people I'm talking to, the more the business is a numbers game, the less I have to press any one prospect to do something, the more I can undersell...and know that I'll get my share of the good people...who respond to me because I undersell. It's an upward spiral; success feeds on itself and begets more success.

And, even though I have to prospect more people, I find I have more than enough energy to do so. Why? Because, when I'm practicing underselling as a form of moral leadership, I'm energized by the pride I take in my work. Being the kind of person you always wanted to be increases rather than depletes your energy!

Thus, in the final analysis, underselling is great for the clients...but even better for you.

Core Beliefs Of The Twenty-First Century Asset Gatherer

It seems very fitting, as this book draws to a close, to go out on a high note. And this article is drawn from one of the highest notes of my career.

In 1994, the International Association for Financial Planning invited me to give the speech at the closing general session of its annual Convention in Boston. This slot had been occupied, in earlier years, by such luminaries as British prime minister Edward Heath and money management superstar Mario Gabelli.

I felt (and continue to feel) very honored to have been given this opportunity, and I felt I owed 'em a real stemwinder. "The Core Beliefs of the Twenty-First Century Asset Gatherer" got a standing ovation. (A tape of the speech is available from the IAFP, if you want to hear it as well as read it.) And, even in print, I think it retains a lot of its effect.

You'll recognize a lot of the themes in this piece from previous articles, but I hope you'll find this a new and useful synthesis of those themes, as well as of some new ones (most notably the concept of the One Thousand Families).

The talk ends this book as it began—on a note of the most deeply-felt long-term bullishness. "NOTE THAT I SAID LONG-TERM BULLISH. ABOUT THE NEXT 15%-20% MOVE, WE MAKE NO GUESSES. YOU SEE, THE 21ST-CENTURY ASSET GATHERER IS EXCUSED FROM KNOWING WHICH WAY THE NEXT 20% MOVE WILL GO. **BECAUSE WE KNOW WHICH WAY THE NEXT 100% MOVE WILL GO.**"

Core Beliefs Of The Twenty-First Century Asset Gatherer

Twenty-first century client relationships—the ones that really endure and enrich both parties—will be those based on shared beliefs, rather than on the transfer of information. So, we professionals will have to base our careers increasingly on our belief system.

Those systems need to be clear, consistent and deeply felt by us, if they are to resonate in like-minded prospective clients. Before a prospect can understand what he's buying, he has to understand who he's buying. A relationship based on the performance of investments is no relationship at all, and must ultimately end badly. But a relationship based on faith in a financial advisor can last a lifetime.

I believe that the truly world-class asset gatherer is approaching the 21st century with a set of 10 core beliefs. You may be more conscious of some of these beliefs than of others, but, if you're going to be one of the real winners, they're all in there, waiting for you to show them to your clients and prospective clients.

1. **The 21st-century asset gatherer is energized, above all, by the amount of good he or she can do**. You and I can do as much good for American families as any other professional, and far more than some whose function is generally more highly thought of than ours.

When you get sick, you go to a doctor, who commences to fight a battle on your behalf, using all his powers. And perhaps, today, he wins that battle. But, in the end, he must lose the war. The medical professional fights a glorious holding action, but his victories are never final.

The war we wage—the struggle for the attainment of real wealth—can not only be won, but that victory can and should transcend death. If our clients heed our counsel, they can become wealthy. Then, if their heirs continue to follow our advice, the family's wealth can continue to accrete, perhaps for generations.

The investment professional's core belief in his or her own capacity for good is what keeps the winner going in the face of adversity and rejection. It is, in that sense, the first and most important of these 10 beliefs.

2. We must know that, in the 21st century as never before, our clients will have to believe in us, because they won't be able to understand us. As markets, tax laws and financial products and strategies grow ever more complex, clients will become less and less able to comprehend what we *know*, and will therefore have to connect more fully with what we *believe*.

Knowledge is about answers, but your beliefs govern the way you're framing the questions. And if you don't have the questions framed right, the answers you get are going to be all wrong anyway.

3. We believe that the primary risk in 21st-century financial life will not be losing one's money, but outliving it. Risk has changed, because life has changed. The 20th century probably saw the end of the equation between retirement and destitution, with the advent of social security, the maturing of the private pension system, and the passage of ERISA.

In the past, retirees lived by spending their savings, i.e., all their principal. In the future, we will be trying to live on our income, while preserving the principal for our heirs. Without professional help, most folks won't make it. That's because they'll continue to define risk and safety in 20th-century terms: purely as a function of principal.

This is the classic example of getting the answers wrong because the questions aren't framed right. Only when America zero-bases this issue (which, without our help, they won't do until it's far too late) can the real issue—purchasing power—become evident. Only then will Americans see that, long term, they have to be owners, not loaners.

Suppose that all you did from now to the end of your career was to cause one thousand American families, with average investable assets of $250,000, to define risk and safety primarily as purchasing power. You would (a) do an incalculable amount of good, (b) become a gazillionaire, and (c) go straight to heaven when you die.

4. **We believe our mission is to turn savers into investors**. An investor is a person who looks forward, into the future, with faith. He observes the course of human history—especially American history—and detects a constant, and now rapidly accelerating, curve of progress. He notes the tendency of shares of great businesses to experience tremendous growth of dividends and (therefore) market value.

A saver looks back, into the past, with fear. He has lost sight of that inexorable curve of progress, because he's obsessed with one particular 20th-century seismic anomaly, which bent (but ultimately didn't break) that curve: the so-called Great Depression. He doesn't want to own anything (including, most days, his house). He wants to lend: short-term, and "guaranteed." (A modest proposal, to snap the American saver out of his catatonic state: phase out the FDIC. But I digress.)

But the shorter-term and more "guaranteed" he lends, the more his purchasing power bleeds away into the sand—after one accounts (as the saver never does) for inflation and taxes. By investing (that is, by letting his principal fluctuate, with faith that time and diversification will vanquish the apocalypse du jour), the American earns real (after-tax, after CPI) returns. Which is like saying: he breathes air. He lives, instead of dying.

Americans will learn this lesson from the contagious faith of the 21st-century asset gatherer...or they'll never learn it at all.

5. **We believe that a neurotic reliance on past investment performance invariably sets the client up to fall**. The Zweig mutual fund group recently published a marketing piece called *Fact vs. Reality*, which, if you haven't seen, you should. The centerpiece to this pamphlet is a study by Morningstar of 219 growth funds for the five years ending May 31 of this year. Morningstar compared the return of the funds themselves (the *investment* return, if you will) with the return of the average invested dollar in the funds during this period (the *investor* return). While the funds' performance aver-

aged 12.5% per year, the average invested dollar earned -2.2%! "Funds did great," the Zweig piece concludes; "people did badly."

Americans buy mutual funds off past performance. This is especially true of those who buy "no-help" funds (previously and erroneously called "no-load" funds). If you buy "help" funds (until recently misnamed "load" funds) you get professional help in seeing that past performance often sends the wrong signal. (Of course, it is possible—and even advisable, in some instances—to buy "no-help" funds from a fee-based asset gatherer, who gives help, and charges money for doing so. But, for at least four out of five Americans, the only really wrong thing to do is to buy "no-help" funds directly from a "no-help" fund company, in such a way as to receive…no help.)

A neurotic reliance on past performance, carried to its logical extreme, makes Americans feel good when they buy a fund which went up spectacularly in the block of time just before they bought it. But I, for one, have always thought it preferable to buy things that performed admirably after I bought them. This often involves buying things that "underperformed" in the block of time before I bought them. Indeed—dare I say it—it sometimes involves buying things that actually went down in the last block of time. Unaided by the 21st-century asset gatherer, Americans will simply never do that. That is our core belief.

You don't just have to buy an investment, you have to keep it, through sickening market declines, and even when some other investment is "outperforming" it. Keeping one's investments, as the Morningstar data show, is virtually impossible for Americans. I believe that, without our help, it's completely impossible.

At the end of your investing lifetime, it won't matter what your funds did, it'll matter what you did. And what you did will be a pure function of the quality of the advice you got—from one caring, competent asset gatherer, and not from any number of magazines.

6. We believe that we make the difference between a family reaching its financial goals and failing to reach them. In our efforts to expand our business we are not so much trying to "qualify" prospective clients as to *disqualify* them. Again, if you can ultimately find one thousand families with $250,000 in investable assets, who see that you make the difference between success and failure, you can accomplish all your goals in this profession. That just means disqualifying all the other families, who don't get it. (This is sometimes mistakenly called "rejection.")

I think that most people intuitively know that they need help. I think, in other words, that the "no-help" fund argument—that you can, unaided, put in place and keep in place a successful lifetime investment program—is counterintuitive.

People believe they can paint their own houses and change their own sparkplugs. But they don't believe they can do their own bypass surgery—nor, I believe, their own lifetime investment program. Then why do they try? Brainwashing, I think. The media has sold them a counterintuitive thesis, in the form of a one-variable equation: the load you don't pay...and never the help you don't get.

You're a salesperson/financial advisor, not a psychiatrist. There are, I assure you, one thousand families out there who are prepared to believe that you make the difference. Disqualify everybody else, and you'll have found them. Don't burn up your energy on those who will not believe. For many are called, but few are chosen. It is a core belief of the 21st-century asset gatherer that he or she is doing the choosing.

7. **We believe that we will never be the low-cost provider of any product or service**. Thank God. The world-class 21st-century asset gatherer gives good advice. Good advice always appears expensive...until you compare it to the terrible cost of bad advice, *much less no advice*. Nothing is more expensive than a no-help fund that a family bails out of when (not if) it's down 25%...because they didn't retain a professional to remind them that, in America, all declines are temporary.

Your price is only an issue when your value is in question. (This is, among other reasons, why you never see a room rate quoted in an ad for Ritz-Carlton hotels.) The 21st-century asset gatherer knows if his or her value is seriously being questioned, the person to whom they are speaking is not from one of the One Thousand Families...and is therefore disqualified.

8. **We believe that a family's investments will become relatively less important than the provisions they may make for the inter-**

generational transfer of its wealth. And that's where we add tremendous value, because our advice can literally be priceless. There is, as far as I know, no such thing as no-load estate planning. And that's going to become the critical issue, as the baby boomers' parents head for the happy hunting ground, and leave them (according to Cornell University) more than 10 trillion dollars over the next two decades.

Investment transactions can be tactical in nature, but intergenerational planning is always strategic. Transactions you can do with 800 numbers, but strategic planning you need to do with people— the best (note: not the lowest cost) people you can find. Once again, we make the difference—if we believe we make the difference.

9. **We know that optimism is simply realism. Fear of the future is counterintuitive**. It's kind of like race hatred: somebody has to teach it to you, because you'd never figure it out for yourself.

Virtually everyone reading this column has had an illness—a flu, pneumonia, some other infection—that 60 years ago would have killed you. MRIs tell us things it would have taken exploratory surgery to find out even 10 years ago. We're making huge advances in both the quality and the length of life. Today, the population over 85 is growing five times faster than the overall U.S. population. And we haven't begun to hear from biotech yet.

Technology? The microprocessor—the entire computer on a chip, mankind's most important invention yet—isn't 25 years old. And the other day, my son went off to school carrying a Texas Instruments TI-30 scientific calculator. It cost $12.88 on sale in Genovese Drug Stores...and it has more computing power than existed on the earth in the year 1950! (But what really galls me is the kid knows how to use the damn thing!)

George Gilder recently wrote that "the technologies of computers and communications will each advance roughly one million-fold in cost effectiveness over the next 10 years." (And what country now leads the world in chip production? No, not Japan; us. As in "U.S.")

Small wonder, then, that Sir John Templeton says, "It has often taken 1,000 years for the standard of living to double in the most advanced countries, yet it may double for the world as a whole in the next 20 years."

10. **Finally, the 21st-century asset gatherer believes that these are the good old days**. Next month, we observe the fifth anniversary of the most important event in world history since the end of WWII—and just possibly the defining event in the rest of our careers as investment professionals.

If you didn't immediately know I meant the destruction of the Berlin Wall (on November 9, 1989), you may be in danger of missing this 10th and last core belief.

It wasn't governments, or treaties, or politicians that tore the wall down. It was people—people, at first, from the east side.

A million people crossed from the east to the west that first weekend. And these were the three most commonly asked questions: "Where is McDonald's? Where can we buy Levi's? Where can we get a Coca-Cola?"

Folks, the war's over; we—the capitalists—won. For, make no mistake about it, the fall of communism was an economic, and not primarily an ideological, victory. In the end, democracy didn't beat totalitarianism so much as capitalism beat socialism. And the curtain is just now going up on the first truly global capitalist revolution. That's why the 21st-century asset gatherer has never been as long-term bullish as he or she is today.

Note that I said long-term bullish. About the next 15%-20% move, we make no guesses. You see, the 21st-century asset gatherer is excused from knowing which way the next 20% move will go. Because we know which way the next 100% move will go. And, deep in your heart, so do you.

Now, go tell the American people.

About the Author

Nick Murray is a 28-year veteran in the field of investment sales and marketing.

His book, *Serious Money: The Art of Marketing Mutual Funds*, is the all-time best-selling book on the investment sales process. *Serious Money* is in use by stockbrokers, life insurance agents, financial planners and bank investment representatives throughout the English-speaking world. The book is now in its sixth printing, with over 100,000 copies in print.

Nick is one of the financial services industry's most popular speakers. He is the only person ever to serve as keynote speaker at the major financial planning conventions in the United States, England and Australia.

Although Nick has done some things in his life of which he is not entirely proud, at least he has never given a motivational speech. He finds that this is something to cling to as he grows older.

Nick Murray is computer illiterate, does not own a scientific calculator, and could not explain the concept of standard deviation to save his life.

NOTES

NOTES

NOTES

NOTES